MADE
IN
CHELSEA

LIFE AND STYLE ESSENTIALS

TIM RANDALL

CONTENTS

TAKE ME
TO CHELSEA

WELCOME TO
CHELSEA

It's the London borough that has become a playground for the capital's glamorous young socialites and a hotbed of love-triangles, posh pardies and oh-so-awkward silences. This book is a celebration of *Made in Chelsea* in all its glory – the gang have exclusively shared their thoughts on everything from dating dilemmas and party survival tips to fashion faux pas and their favourite SW1 hangouts. If you need a bit more Binky, Jamie and Spencer in your existence, this is your must-have guide to living life the Chelsea way...

LONDON

Chelsea (n) [chel-see]
(place name) A fashionable residential district
on the north bank of the River Thames, in
the Royal Borough of Kensington and Chelsea.

ETIQUETTE
ESSENTIALS

MEETING AND GREETING

To kiss or not to kiss? One kiss or two? Bear hug or a mid-air mwah, mwah? Social etiquette can be a minefield of awkwardness but in Chelsea the rules couldn't be simpler. You kiss hello on two cheeks and you kiss goodbye on two cheeks. Never once.

STEP I
FEIGN ENTHUSIASM AT SPOTTING YOUR ACQUAINTANCE.
– despite the fact that they may be the last person you want to see. Even if it's your ex's new incredibly beautiful girlfriend, you must appear delighted to see her.

STEP 2
POSITION YOURSELF.
As you lean in, place your left hand on their right shoulder or upper arm. Always keep hands above the waist.

STEP 3
OFFER YOUR RIGHT
CHEEK FOLLOWED BY
YOUR LEFT CHEEK.

Always brush or kiss cheeks.
Air-kissing is a social faux pas
and looks ridiculous.

Top Tips

★ **Lip-locks** ★
Attempting a smooch as
a social greeting is a major
faux pas and just plain awkward.
These are reserved for lovers
and some families who greet
each other with a brisk
peck on the lips.

★ ★ ★

STEP 4
MAKE A DISCREET
KISSING SOUND
AS YOU EMBRACE.

An ear-deafening mwah
bellowed into the lobe of
your companion is a no-no.
Avoid looking as if you're
trying too hard – always social-
kiss with a blasé confidence
and charm. Don't linger
and keep it swift.

STEP 5
END WITH
A COMPLIMENT.

End with a compliment.
Boys should inform girls
that they look amazing and
girls should flatter female
acquaintances (whether
they mean it or not). These
compliments should be accepted
as statement of fact with a
simple thank you. Do not attempt
false modesty. In Chelsea no
one feigns surprise at being
complimented – you *know*
you look great. Own it.

BOIS BASICS

★

Ever had your open arms met with a frosty outstretched hand?
Awkward! Here are three socially acceptable men braces
and advice on how to use them...

THE TRAD HANDSHAKE

Make sure your grip is firm
and friendly. You don't want to
appear a wet fish, but you don't
want to crush the other person's
hand either. This isn't a willy-
waggling competition. Keep it
brisk – two thrusts and you're
done. Suitable for first-time
introductions, formal occasions
and for your dad – who'd freak
at anything more touchy-feely.

THE MAN-HUG

One arm is positioned over
your pal's shoulder, the other
is placed below his opposite
shoulder. Hold briefly and give
a few short taps on the back,
but avoid pounding their spine
as if you're carrying out a reverse
Heimlich. To be used when
feeling particularly celebratory
or reuniting with The Bois after
a St Barts-based separation.

THE BRO-SHAKE

Outstretch your right hand and grasp their right hand at a vertical angle as if you're about to arm-wrestle. Swing in towards them so that your chests touch briefly. This motion is completed with your left hand reaching around their right shoulder to give two open-palmed slaps. Release your hand grip to end the greeting. For your inner circle – if extended to a newbie it will be taken as a sign of acceptance.

THE FIST-BUMP

If it's workin' for Obama, then it's good enough for Jamie and Spencer. Make sure your clenched hand is at an equal height to your pal's, then gently bump fists for a second before pulling away.

Top Tip

★ **The hand-grasp** ★

An alternative stance when leaning in for a social kiss is to clutch the other person's hands at chest height. This appears friendly, but can act as a useful barrier to prevent the other person becoming physically close. Ideal for fending off drunk suitors or unpredictable relations.

★ ★ ★

"The worst thing is when you go for the handshake and someone else goes for the hug and your hand ends up in their stomach. I get through it by dominating the situation and making it very clear that I am going for the handshake, the hug or the two kisses. The secret is to make your intentions clear from the outset rather than waiting for a last-minute decision. It's like a penalty shoot-out – you have to take aim and go for it."

JAMIE

Here's

BINKY FELSTEAD

'I love the feeling of freedom
you get being out in the countryside
on your horse.'

I'm a country girl at heart... I had a fun outdoorsy childhood.
I'd get up every morning and muck out the horses. My last horse
was called Toddy and we used to do lots of events and horse shows
together. I don't ride as much now, as I'm in London most of the
time, but I go back home to East Sussex, to my mum's, and I get on
a horse occasionally, just to clear my head. I love the fresh air and the
feeling of freedom you get from being out in the countryside on your
horse. That's when I can totally switch off. When I get married and
have kids, I will definitely get horses so that they can ride and have
the same kind of country childhood that I did.

My real name is Alexandra... everybody always asks me where
the name Binky comes from and I still don't really know the answer.
I've asked my mum, and she thinks it was a mixture of when I was
small and bad, so a combination of bad and dinky!

My flowing locks are extensions... I actually used to have real
hair like this, but I stupidly cut it all off when I was younger. My mum's
never forgiven me. I'm trying to get it to grow back, so that's why
I've got these in, and it ensures that it doesn't get damaged too
much when I'm having it styled for shoots.

My guilty pleasure... Chicken jalfrezi after a night out, and
Geordie Shore. It's compulsive viewing!

Here's

JAMIE LAING

'One of my school reports said, "getting cross with Jamie is like drowning puppies".'

My great-great grandfather invented the Jaffa Cake... and I've always loved sweets, but I was never given pocket money, so I was never able to go and buy them. I used to steal from our sweetie jar instead. I was only allowed white chocolate because other sweets made me too hyper.

Boarding school bored me... one of my end-of-year reports said, 'getting cross with Jamie is like drowning puppies'. I charmed all the teachers yet did no work ever. Boarding school is a lot of fun because it's basically hanging out with your mates all the time, but the repetition of life at my school, nearly killed me. I remember when I left saying I'd rather do a year in jail than spend another 12 months there.

We always try and play pranks on each other... I'd have to say that the three Lost Bois – me, Francis and Proudlock, probably are the naughtiest. We're always trying to put each other off! We're going to release a song. We've even made a funny, cheesy 90s boy band style video.

The biggest misconception about me... is I'm not that bright. But I'm sharper than people think. I'm kind of like the Boris Johnson of sweets. I'm perceived as the party boy who doesn't really do much, but I have got a brain and I am one of the few people in the cast who has set up a vaguely successful business. I thought, what do I love? Well, I love sweets, I love fashion and I love girls, so I put them together and I created the Candy Kittens concept.

CHELSEA
DATING

DATING
THE CHELSEA WAY

Want to know how to give your love life the Chelsea lift it needs? Follow our simple guide for all your dating needs…

ASKING FOR A DATE…

Remember, it's never a 'date' at first. A simple 'we should hang out sometime' gets the message across loud and clear. Never appear desperate – you don't need that drink, but it'd be, like, kind of fun if it happened. Unless you can pull off the cheeky-chappie Jamie vibe, steer clear of cheesy chat-up lines such as 'Is it hot in here or is it just you?' A Chelsea girl is more likely to give you the cold shoulder than fall into your arms with that kind of technique.

"Choose somewhere different for a date, like the Natural History Museum or the aquarium – the conversation will flow easily and you'll learn about something else as well as each other." **JAMIE**

THE FIRST DATE...

When you're ready to take socialising into the dating arena, your choice of venue speaks volumes and a warm pint down the Dog & Duck will simply not do. If the budget allows, think big – lunch in Paris is standard, but champagne and oysters will get similar results.

No one wants to sit in a stuffy restaurant making small talk over endless courses – try a more fun dining experience. Mexican! Peruvian! Ribs! Browsing the menu will kick-start conversation, ensuring there'll be none of those oh-so-awkward *Made in Chelsea* silences. See our foodie first date venue suggestions on page 202.

★ ★ ★ ★ ★

DO
Think outside the box.
Jamie took Binky golfing – sometimes random can be endearing.

DON'T
Invite your mates along.
When Jamie's 'Bois' crashed the date, it went from a hole-in-one to a bunker-bound flop.

"Going to the cinema on a first date is the worst. You spend two hours with a person, but don't find out a thing about them because you can't speak. Overriding all of that is the panic that they might try and cop a feel." OLIVIA

DRESSING FOR SUCCESS

★

You've only got one chance to make a first impression...

THINK UNDERSTATED GLAM
The best dress is never revealed on date one. Don't overcomplicate your look in a bid to impress.

BE COMFORTABLE
Road-test your outfit beforehand. You don't want to be squirming all night in a bodycon dress you can't sit down in.

DRESS FOR THE OCCASION
Don't up-style for dinner at Nobu if the date's a breezy picnic in Courtfield Gardens.

KEEP HAIR AND MAKE-UP NATURAL
But with a hint of glamour. Chelsea boys don't want a girlfriend with a face painted on like a clown.

AND FOR THE BOYS...
Shoes, shoes, shoes. Get the footwear right with a smart pair of brogues or chukka boots and you've scored points before you've even said hello. Stick to a cool fitted shirt and avoid baggy slogan tops. Don't overdo the cologne, check your hair and breath, make sure your fingernails are clean and clipped – and you're good to go!

'Girls who turn up caked in make-up just kill me. If I feel as if I'm sitting opposite a Barbie, I just want to get the next cab home.' **ANDY**

'Bad shoes, dirty nails and grubby teeth and ears are a real turn-off. Also, guys who wear hats on a date. Who wants to date someone wearing a beanie?' **OLIVIA**

'Don't dress for the guy you're seeing. Don't get your boobs out. Don't get your legs out. Yes, on the second date you can sex it up a bit – but that doesn't mean you have to reveal body parts. Keep the mystery.' **ROSIE**

'A girl who reveals too much skin is a turn-off. I want to focus on the person not the body, initially. The body can come later!' **JAMIE**

DATING DOS AND DON'TS

DO

★

HAVE FUN AND ENJOY YOURSELF

STEVIE: 'A girl who's chatty and confident in her own skin is always attractive.'

★

SHARE A PUD

OLLIE: 'It's so sensual. But don't feed each other – that's way too much on a first date!'

★

BE YOURSELF

MILLIE: 'Stay true to who you are – don't suddenly change your personality to suit the date.'

★

CHECK YOUR BREATH

SPENCER: 'If your breath reeks, you can kiss goodbye to that first-date snog.'

★

BE ENTHUSIASTIC

OLIVIA: 'Whether it's travel, a hobby or a sport, talking about a passion is a real turn-on.'

★

PUT YOUR PHONE ON SILENT

BINKY: 'Give them your full attention. You can always take a sneaky peek at your messages when they pop to the loo.'

★

MIND YOUR MANNERS

VICTORIA: 'Be courteous to your date and polite to staff. Always leave a good tip – it shows you have generosity of spirit.'

DON'T

GET SOZZLED

ROSIE: 'Slurring your words and slumping forward in your seat isn't a good look.'

BE A SLOB

ANDY: 'If someone ate with their mouth open, I don't think I'd be able to last the whole date.'

TALK ABOUT AN EX

OLIVIA: 'It's a tell-tale sign you aren't over them. A first date should be bright and breezy – you shouldn't feel like someone's shrink!'

INTERVIEW YOUR DATE

STEVIE: 'I wouldn't want someone constantly firing questions at me, but at the same time you don't want someone who's monosyllabic either.'

BE A SHOW-OFF

CHESKA: 'There's a fine line between confidence and arrogance. Guys who boast about their trust fund and Daddy's yacht are such a turn-off.'

DUMB DOWN

FRANCIS: 'I don't like anti-intellectuals, people who don't care about learning. I like people who respect themselves and want to be the best person they can be.'

BE TOO TOUCHY-FEELY

FRANCESCA: 'Nobody wants to be mauled and it will only make the other person uncomfortable. Remember: respect personal space!'

BE TOO KEEN

FRANCESCA: 'Don't gush and overcompliment – you'll come across as desperate.'

CHESKA'S GUIDE TO FLIRTING

Your body language can say more than words...

★

'Maintain eye contact but don't
stare too manically or you'll
scare them off.'

★

'Open up your body, lean
in towards your date and keep
those arms unfolded.'

★

'Make contact; touch their hand
occasionally as you chat. But footsie
under the table is a no-no.'

★

'Show those pearly whites – nothing
says "I like you" more than
a genuine smile!'

WHO PAYS THE BILL?

As a general rule, the person who asks for the date pays for it. You may agree to split the bill, but when someone else has suggested the date, you are not obliged to do so.

★

'If a guy tried to make me pick up the bill on a first date, I would never see him again. I'm very old-fashioned like that.'

VICTORIA

★

'On the first date the guy always pays for the girl. A couple of dates in I would wait to see if she offered. If she didn't, I would dump her – nobody wants to date a gold-digger.'

ANDY

★

'A girl should always offer to pay and it's up to the boy whether he accepts. I'm the kind of person that doesn't like to feel indebted to a guy.'

ROSIE

AWKWARD!

★

The first dates from hell...

'I went for dinner with a guy who was good-looking but had really bad halitosis – I could smell it across the table. It was so disgusting I wanted to throw up. I want to throw up now just thinking about it.' **VICTORIA**

'A girl once told me she used to drink her cat's milk. Her mum thought that was really cute, so she'd put this girl's milk in the cat bowl too. That was a pretty creepy, weird conversation. I didn't see her again.' **FRANCIS**

'As a nervous 16-year-old, I sweated through the grey t-shirt I was wearing. It started under my arms and began to meet in the middle. I was literally sopping wet. I had to go to the bathroom, splash loads of water over myself and pretend the tap had broken and soaked me.' **JAMIE**

'I formed a relationship with a guy online and thought we were in love. When I actually met him in real life, it turned out he was revolting. I then spilt tomato sauce all the way down my top, and when I wiped water on, it went see-through. I broke up with him by text about two hours after that happened.' **LUCY**

'I dated a really bad kisser. I'd quite liked her beforehand, but then we kissed and it was like – Jesus Christ! It turned me off so much I didn't know what to do. It was like I'd just caught a fish and it was flapping around on the inside of my mouth. I couldn't face a second date after that.' **ANDY**

HOOKING UP...

Keep it safe and keep it discreet – a good Chelsea boy would never kiss and tell. Don't tweet, Facebook or blog your nocturnal naughtiness for the world to discuss. Privacy and decorum is key.

BECOMING AN ITEM...

When you're ready for The Discussion, make sure you're clear on the rules. Being exclusive means boyfriend and girlfriend and no room for ambiguity. If they try to keep it vague, you'd better show them the door. Exclusivity means a subtle revamp of your Facebook relationship status, no text flirting with others, no matter how innocent it is, and an agreement not to share a hot tub in Verbier with anyone vaguely attractive.

KEEPING THE SPARK...

You need to keep the magic alive, and that means never getting complacent. If the fun times dry up and you're noticing your other half would rather be out on lash with their mates (à la Louise and Spencer), you're doing something very wrong. Keep one night a week just for you, plan trips away and never, ever let your other half see you wearing loungewear.

66My most embarrassing *Made in Chelsea* moment? Telling Andy that I fancied him when he was already planning to dump me. Awkward! 99

FRANCESCA

Top Tips

★ Organise date nights ★
make quality time for yourselves
without the hangers-on.

★ Be spontaneous ★
break the routine and book
that last-minute Eurostar
to Paris right now.

★ Don't nag ★
nothing screams unsexy like bitching
at each other about emptying the
bin or how long it has taken you
to get ready.

★ Surprises ★
whether it's champers in bed,
a romantic Post-it note on the
fridge or a homemade cupcake,
small gestures can make your
heart soar!

★ ★ ★

ALFRESCO AMOUR

★

*Using those puppy-dog eyes to his best advantage,
it was while picnicking in Courtfield Gardens
that loved-up Spencer told Lucy Watson
he was falling for her, proving just how romantic
a surprise picnic can be, whether it's for
a first date or as a way to keep the spark alive.*

So, what's the secret of the perfect
picnic? 'You need to find a good
spot under a nice big tree that's
not too crowded,' suggests Spencer.
'A hamper full of goodies from
Fortnum & Mason would work
really well, as would a decent bottle
of Prosecco. But at the risk of
sounding like a total cheese-ball,
the most important thing about
a romantic picnic is the person
you're with...'

A FINE ROMANCE

★

The way to a Chelsea girl's heart...

'After a Valentine's meal out, I arrived back at my boyfriend's flat and our song ('I Just Called To Say I Love You') was already playing. There were candles everywhere and a trail of rose petals leading to the bedroom. We had this thing where I called him my rock and he called me his seashell, and by the bedroom door was a little jewellery box – inside was a seashell he'd had cast in silver and made into a necklace.' **CHESKA**

'There was a guy at uni who brought me flowers every day for three months. He'd also turn up each day to take me to classes in his car. His persistence paid off, we started dating and for my 21st he bought me one thousand roses.' **VICTORIA**

'I've had lots of gifts and grand gestures, but romance isn't about material things; it's about actions. The most romantic thing someone has done for me is looking after me when I'm unwell. I've been throwing my guts up crying and my boyfriend would hold my hair and clean up my sick. Being looked after when you're ill shows just how much they love you.' **LUCY**

SPOTTING THE PROBLEMS...

The tell-tale signs to look out for...

Their ex refuses to accept defeat and
totally disappear from the world.

★

They won't introduce you to their friends.

★

The word 'boyfriend' or 'girlfriend' sticks
in their throat like a mouthful of cotton wool.

★

They won't chuck out their gay porn stash.

★

They're planning a skiing holiday,
barn dance or masked ball
and you've yet to receive an invitation.

★

*If any of the above apply, get in there first
and send them packing back to Mahiki's singles
night quicker than you can sing 'We are never,
ever, ever, getting back together'.*

CHEATING...

It does happen, let's be honest. But keep things classy. If you've done the dirty, you'd better fess up to your wrongdoings on your own terms. Chinese whispers make a bad situation even worse and the last thing you need is a Francis vs Spenny vs Millie showdown in public. But on the other hand, revenge is a dish best served cold, and if you find out you've been the victim of a philandering partner, make sure they know how mad you are. A vodka martini in the face should get the message across.

THE TRICKY LOVE-TRIANGLE ISSUE...

Whether you're stuck in the middle or you're the third wheel, you'd better keep your eyes peeled for potentially spiky situations when two's company becomes a crowded three. Your partner's ex rearing their ugly head is the most common of all causes, so you'd better be quick to remind your other half what dampened the former flame in the first place if you want to avoid any boomerang dating. Meanwhile, if your own ghost of hooking-up past makes a reappearance, keep in mind the mantra, 'never look back'. Don't recycle your dates – vintage is a concept best kept on the catwalk.

Top tip

If you've cheated on your girlfriend in your girlfriend's bed (gross, Spencer), then man-up and take your punishment on the chin. And please tell us that you changed the sheets.

★ ★ ★

45

HOW TO SPOT A LOVE CHEAT

★

1 He's cheated before. Previous flings are the most reliable predictor of future dodgy behaviour.

2 He's an emotionless narcissist. Boys who cheat are only focused on one thing – themselves.

3 He eagerly scrawls down relationship advice every time his idol Spencer appears on screen.

SECOND CHANCES?

Research shows that 65 per cent of unfaithful couples end up remaining together and there are several circumstances in which granting a second chance is allowed. Firstly, the wronged party must be apologetic and grovelling to the point of near-public humiliation. Anything less is unacceptable. And secondly, if you've been equally as awful to them, then you should probably call it evens and realise you're as bad as each other and it's fate.

BREAKING UP...

There's always a time to wave goodbye; don't oversentimentalise it. Arrange to speak face to face – text dumping is socially obnoxious, as is telling everyone else you know it's over (including tweeting all your followers) before actually telling the person yourself. Make sure you're doing the dumping in a public place where there's less likelihood of drama, raised voices or waterworks. If they do start bawling, don't go back on your word. Give your reasons sensitively without crushing their heart – they are undoubtedly going to be gutted, so try to soften with a compliment ('you're too good for me', 'you're an amazing person, but I'm not ready…'). Once the deed is done, be sure to lay low and, out of decency and self-respect, avoid going straight out and pulling someone on the same night. The rebound snog is rarely a high-quality catch anyway.

TEXTBOOK DUMPING

Lucy Watson ditched Andy at dinner before they'd even ordered their aperitif, thus saving them time and money.

DUMPING DISASTER

Spencer telling Louise one of the reasons he was dumping her was her relentless forgiveness of his cheating. Ouch – uncalled for!

> **"Someone is always going to get hurt. So in the same way as peeling off a plaster, you've got to make breaking up as quick and as painless as possible."**
> **FRANCIS**

STAYING FRIENDS WITH YOUR EX...

It's easier all round if you can stay on speaking terms with your ex. Unless you're planning to box them up and ship them out to Outer Mongolia, you're bound to run into them. When you do, adopt a poised, unflinching image of cool. A simple 'Hi, how are things going?' will keep things civil and polite. There's nothing to be gained by being that screeching harridan who can't be in the same room as her ex. In the end, you'll miss out on the best party invites through your own inability to keep it friendly, even if it is fake.

TIPS FOR A DIGNIFIED ENDING

★

Choose the right time – don't
do it on their birthday or
at Christmas, otherwise that
day will be forever marred by
memories of your ditching.

★

Choose the right place – unlike
Ollie, who broke up with
Gabriella whilst stranded
in the middle of the Thames
at Francis's boat party.

★

Word it well – explain why
the relationship isn't working
for you and focus on how you
feel rather than listing their faults.
Express regret and wish them
well for the future.

THE FRIENDLY FAKE-OUT

1 Smile. Use every ounce of facial strength not to let that mouth curl into a snarl.

2 Do a quick once-over up and down with the eyes to ascertain whether they've been on the heartbreak diet or veered towards comfort eating.

3 Make small talk. Perhaps drop in a passive-aggressive comment about the new guy you're dating…

4 …then as quick as you can, GET OUT of there and move on to the next person. Do not linger and be careful not to trip, fall or shake with fury at having to be in the same room as them.

5 Once home, phone, text, email your friends and let it all out. Maybe have a glass of rosé to take the edge off?

CAN YOU STAY FRIENDS WITH AN EX?

FOR
SPENCER

AGAINST
LUCY

'I'm friends with all my exes and I pride myself on that. Louise and I are even getting there, which is quite an achievement. If you've loved someone in the past, I don't see why you have to start hating them just because the relationship didn't work out. I find it quite easy to go straight back to being mates. I'm now close friends with both Funda and Caggie, because as time passes, so do the problems. If we're both over it – what's the issue?'

'I can't do it. I'm too black and white. I think it's fine to be friends with someone you weren't in love with – like me and Andy, because that was very short-lived. But I've been in love three times and I haven't spoken to any of them since. I find when I break up with people they still want to be with me, so I have to cut them out of my life. If you've been in love, those feelings never die, so it's inappropriate to spend time together because you're effectively leading them on.'

★

See what the wisest woman in Chelsea – Binky's mum, Janey Felstead – has to say about this and other relationship dilemmas on page 56.

ARE YOU A PLAYER?

★

When it comes to romance and dating, the Chelsea lot are
all over it. But how do your moves compare to theirs?

★ **YOU WANT TO HOOK UP WITH A GUY WHO'S JUST SPLIT UP**
WITH HIS GIRLFRIEND – SOMEONE YOU'VE NEVER LIKED. DO YOU…
A) Tell everyone and their handbag-dog that you fancy him and
wait for the gossips to do the legwork for you.
B) Leave a faux-respectful pause before texting about a date.
C) Make sure you get with him at the first possible opportunity.

★ **THERE ARE RUMOURS THAT YOUR BEST MATE'S BLOKE HAS**
SLEPT WITH SOMEONE BEHIND HER BACK. DO YOU…
A) Waste a perfectly good vodka martini by throwing it in his face.
B) Do some digging, present the evidence and leave her to deal with it.
C) Get your mum and your best mates' two mums to confront the
guy at lunch and get up in his grill.

★ **YOU'RE AWAY WITH THE BOIS AND HAVE INVITED A FEW**
HOT GIRLS, BUT NOT YOUR DEVOTED GIRLFRIEND. DO YOU…
A) Get totally wasted in a hot tub and kiss your flirty companion,
forgetting that she'll make sure your girlfriend finds out.
B) Get a bit flirty, but certainly no PDAs – you're attached.
C) Hope that whatever happens on holiday stays on holiday
and get with anyone you can. Sick!

★ **YOUR SHADY SNAKE OF A BOYFRIEND DUMPS YOU AND**
YOU'RE IN BITS. HOW DO YOU MOVE ON WITH YOUR LIFE?
A) Stalk the ex at every party going and ruin any chance
he's got of hooking up #revengeissweet.

B) Serious amounts of gymmage + serious shopping with the girls = looking seriously good. See ya!

C) Ignore the fact that he's treated you terribly and that your friends hate him and carry on sleeping with him in secret.

★ **WHILE YOUR GIRLFRIEND IS AWAY YOU GET WITH SOMEONE IN HER BED. WHEN SHE HEARS ABOUT IT YOU...**

A) Deny, deny, deny!

B) Come clean and beg for forgiveness, pleading insanity.

C) Dump her to avoid hassle, then admit to it weeks later.

★ **YOU'RE IN DUBAI WITH A MIXED GROUP OF FRIENDS. WHILE YOU'RE THERE A MATE HOOKS UP WITH ANOTHER MATE'S GIRLFRIEND. DO YOU...**

A) Stay well out of it – it's not your problem, bro.

B) Break the Bois code and call home straightaway.

C) Demand your mate does the right thing and confesses.

★ **YOU MOVE BACK HOME AFTER LIVING ABROAD AND INSTANTLY FEEL A VIBE WITH AN OLD FRIEND, BUT DRUNKENLY KISS HIS MATE. DO YOU...**

A) Get hangover paranoia and write them both off #awkward.

B) Blame it on the copious vodka shots and pretend it never happened.

C) Carry on with the best mate while pining for the crush, until he starts seeing someone. Then make your move.

★ **YOUR GIRLFRIEND IS GETTING COSY AT YOUR FLAT. WHILE YOU'RE OUT SHE REARRANGES YOUR DVDS AND FINDS SOME GAY PORN. DO YOU...**

A) Leave it to your best mate to break it to her that you're bisexual.

B) Admit you swing both ways and ask if she fancies a threesome.

C) Go all wide-eyed and gulpy as you try to pretend the films are someone else's.

MOSTLY AS

You are a player! When it comes to dating you're all about quantity not quality. Getting tied down is for losers! Fancy a drink?

MOSTLY BS

Your mum would be proud. Well done on having impeccable manners with morals to match. (You wouldn't survive a hot minute in Chelsea.)

MOSTLY CS

You're an all-rounder – a healthy mix of totally devious and utterly charming. Perfect for stealth-pulling, parent-impressing and pants-offing!

ASK BINKY'S MUM

The wisest woman in Chelsea – aka Janey Felstead – tackles your awkward relationship dilemmas...

★ *Dear Binky's mum. I'm going to a party and my ex will be there with his new girlfriend, i.e. the woman he left me for. How can I deal with the situation without thumping him or her?*

The best way is to stand tall, pretend you don't care and bribe an exceptionally good-looking male friend to be your date. They'll understand the task at hand and there'll be no complications afterwards. Do make sure they are unknown to your ex. It's so embarrassing to get discovered!

★ *Dear Binky's mum. I cheat on my girlfriends and blame them when I get found out. I don't know why I do it. Am I a bad person?*

Yes, I think you sound like a total pillock. My advice to you is to remember that karma does exist and what goes around comes around. It's never too late to change your ways for the greater good.

★ *Dear Binky's mum. I've barely started dating a guy and already his overprotective ex has warned me off him. How can I get her off my back?*

Firstly, remember she is his ex and the reason for that is she was probably a total nightmare. Take a chill pill; he wants you right now. Life goes on and people have to cope with that.

★ *Dear Binky's mum. I have just discovered that my boyfriend is sleeping with half the girls in Chelsea. I'd like to plot a suitable revenge. Any suggestions?*

You must remember that revenge is a dish best served cold. If I were you, I'd be devious in my actions. Get some reliable friends to help you find a delish ladyboy to set him up with, then be there with a camera at the vital moment. This, of course, will take some planning and expense – but frankly nothing worth having is ever cheap and you can get the most wonderful things with the help of American Express.

★ *Dear Binky's mum. I have been known to slap boys and throw drinks in their faces. Do I have anger issues?*

No, not necessarily. But perhaps you were the sort of girl who got her own way from a young age. I think you are carrying this forward now, and my advice to you would be to take your foot off the pedal and relax.

★ *Dear Binky's mum. I found a stash of gay porn in my boyfriend's flat. What should I do?*

Well, if you want the truth RUN. Unless you look like the back end of a No 22 bus, I'm sure you can find yourself someone else. This chap needs to find some space to discover what he really wants, and you giving him this can be looked upon as an act of extreme kindness.

★ *Dear Binky's mum. My ex seems to be everywhere I go as we're in the same circle of friends. Is it possible to stay mates with an ex?*

Yes, I believe it is possible to stay friends. I don't want to sound too much like a feminist here – but girls, real girls, are intelligent and able. I think if you grit your teeth and accept the fact it may be difficult, then something good will come of it. Such as some other truly lovely man

noticing your adult approach and appreciating it – they are out there, and for every foot there's a shoe!

Also watch out for...

GIRLY-GIRLS

The girl who takes being girly to the extreme is very irritating and does nothing for womenkind. They float around and flutter their eyelashes and expect boys to pander to their every whim. These girls have the ability to turn quite nasty if they don't get their way and can cry at the drop of a hat. Boys, beware of these types – they're often the ones who later become bunny boilers!

LITTLE BOYS

A man at 23 is a bit like a girl at 15 – so juvenile. In times of war men were forced to grow up early, work and be responsible, but now they're taking much longer to mature. These Chelsea boys may look hot, but the simple fact is their bodies have got there before their heads. Enjoy your dalliances with them, but don't expect too much – remember, their mental age is still in the playground!

Here's

VICTORIA BAKER-HARBER

'People expect me to be
a stone-cold bitch – they're always
surprised that I'm nice.'

I hated boarding school … and the teachers hated me too. I didn't fit in and the worst thing about when you start is that you know you're going to be stuck there for at least the next five years. I said to my parents, if you don't get me out of here I'm going to make sure I get into so much trouble that I'll be given no choice but to leave.

I had a tracksuit for every day of the month … I was a bit of a tomboy and used to love Juicy tracksuits. Between the ages of 14 and 17 I would just walk around in black eye make-up and a luminous green Juicy tracksuit. That's all I wore. Can you imagine it? I bit my nails too, then a boyfriend who was six years older told me I had horrible hands, so that kind of stuck. Now I'm a total perfectionist when it comes to my nails and my cuticles.

I love a villain … generally I am fascinated by villain characters in films, especially if they're played by Javier Bardem or Benicio Del Toro. I have been out with lots of villains. Every time. I very rarely get the good guy.

The biggest misconception about me … is people expect me to be a stone-cold bitch or really tough. So when people meet me for the first time, they're always surprised that I'm actually friendly and nice. I'd do anything for my friends. I'd be there at five o'clock in the morning if they needed me and they say I always give good advice – but at the same time I'm not very good at taking it!

Here's

MARK FRANCIS VANDELLI

'My mother dressed me as a sailor
until I was six years old.'

My parents were horrified when I joined **Made in Chelsea**...
my mother told me that if I ever got involved in reality TV that would
be the end of our relationship. My father said the same. They weren't
impressed and we didn't speak for a while. It goes without saying they
eventually forgave me. I'm their only son, I'm hard to forget.

I was chic even as a child... my mother only ever dressed me as
a sailor until I was six years old. She has a Russian background and
it's a Russian tradition to dress little boys in a navy sailor suit. I have
some really nice pictures of me in that when I was tiny. I was quite
cute – much cuter than I am now.

The biggest misconception about me... is that I'm a snob. I'm
not. I just do things my way. People think I'm from another planet
and that I'm out of touch with the real world, but I'm a very grounded
person and I'm a very realistic person. I am in touch with people from
all sorts of different backgrounds and cultures.

I'm always putting my foot in it... I was at a dinner party sitting
with David Beckham and Gordon Ramsay and we were talking about
holidays in Sardinia. I told them I used to spend a couple of idyllic
months in Sardinia every year as a child and David mentioned that he
hadn't been there for a long time. I replied: 'Oh it's lovely, but we sold
our house because these days it's full of footballers and really trashy
celebrities.' The whole table went silent. You could've heard a pin drop.

CHELSEA
FASHION

The Home Counties Hottie
BINKY FELSTEAD

Binks isn't your typical Chelsea fashionista, so don't expect to see her at Dover Street Market combing the rails. That said, she always looks good in a high-street 'I-haven't-tried-at-all' kinda way, with sexy bed hair to accent the casual look. Tending to favour loose-fitting tops, she goes for it on the bottoms, getting those legs out in short skirts and shorts teamed with wedges. As a beauty writer, she knows a thing or two about working it – her make-up is always flawless.

MY STYLE

TOPSHOP
'Who needs designer when you can get everything you need in Topshop. I could literally spend days in there.'
topshop.com

HERMÈS
'I don't spend huge amounts of money on clothes, but I do like expensive bags. The Birkin is amazing.'
hermes.com

PAMPERING

GLO
'For nails, tan, hair, eyelashes. You'll find me in there every week!'
glofulham.com

STYLE ICON

'Blake Lively – she's just really hot and really fit. She's my girl crush!'

★ MY TIP ★

'I don't think you need to cake on the make-up when you are young; save that for when you're old and wrinkly. Mum always says that less is more – and she's right.'

★ MY TIP ★

'Always do your make-up in natural light and keep it simple. Don't mask what you have – enhance it.'

The Vamp
MILLIE MACKINTOSH

Make-up artist Millie is always picture perfect. Adopting a clever mix of designer and high street, pouty Millie nails the ideal look whether she's attending a première, going to a festival or hitting the shops in Bond Street. Rarely seen without a huge tote and shades, the self-confessed fashion junkie makes looking good seem all too easy.

MY STYLE

ALEXANDER MCQUEEN
'The epitome of British fashion. Their red-carpet gowns create the most incredible silhouettes.'
alexandermcqueen.com

D&ME
'I love this shop! Designer and vintage all under one roof.'
dandme.co.uk

AUSTIQUE
'Everything from glamorous pretty fashion to cute jewellery and accessories.'
austique.co.uk

BUTLER & WILSON
'Bold statement costume jewellery.'
butlerandwilson.co.uk

PAMPERING

PERFECT 10
'From waxing to a facial – they bring the spa to your house!'
perfect10mobilebeauty.co.uk

STYLE ICON
'Audrey Hepburn always looked effortlessly chic. I love Brigitte Bardot too – she's a hot mess!'

The Fashion Maven
PHOEBE-LETTICE THOMPSON

Pouty, peroxide and pretty, Phoebe has caught all the Bois' attention. With a nod to 90s grunge, fashion assistant Phoebe doesn't follow the West London pack in the style stakes and is subsequently the edgiest dresser of the Chelsea crowd. More likely to be seen in a sexy shirt, cigarette pants and block-heeled boots than a bodycon dress and strappies, will she encourage others to get on board with the long-forgotten nose ring?

MY STYLE

TOM FORD

'His last collection had so much punch – sculptured fur and great patterns. You just want to roll around in all of it!'
tomford.com

RELLIK

'It's a treasure trove of high-end vintage – everything from Vivienne Westwood to Yves St Laurent.'
relliklondon.co.uk

BEYOND RETRO

'A huge vintage clothing collection for all price ranges. I bought my favourite pair of big clumpy boots there.'
beyondretro.com

THIERRY LASRY

'I have about 80 pairs of sunglasses. Most of them aren't expensive because I end up sitting on them or losing them, but I do have a really cool, chunky Thierry Lasry pair.'
thierrylasry.com

STYLE ICON

'Kate Moss is effortlessly cool. Everyone wants what Kate has!'

★ MY TIP ★

'You can't go wrong with a pair of black jeans, black pointed court shoes or stilettos, a black leather jacket and a white t-shirt. It just works!'

★ **MY TIP** ★

If you're going to
wear an earring, you've
got to own it — wear
it with confidence
and with pride!'

The West London Hipster
OLLIE PROUDLOCK

Very different from a bearded East London hipster, super-clean-shaven fashion designer Prouders is at the cutting edge of where it's at among the guys in conservative Chelsea. Slick, sick and chiselled, the man even coordinates his outfits with his trademark tortoiseshell specs. Skinnies, long necklaces, earrings (multiple, in both ears), tatts, rings and statement t-shirts (ostensibly from his own collection — Serge DeNïmes) make him the most stylish of the Bois by far.

MY STYLE

RALPH LAUREN
'Their stuff is timeless because of the attention to quality and detail.'
ralphlauren.co.uk

ACNE
'The emphasis is on quality and cut. Everything is very subtle and Scandi-cool.'
acnestudios.com

WOLF & BADGER
'They showcase different independent designers, plus really interesting jewellery and accessories.'
wolfandbadger.com

OLIVER SWEENEY
'I designed a high-top trainer and a chukka boot for them. I get such a kick out of seeing people wearing my stuff.'
oliversweeney.com

STYLE ICON
'Johnny Depp has a unique, boho, chilled-out vibe, whereas Pharrell Williams always looks sick and on point.'

The Modern English Rose
ROSIE FORTESCUE

Eschewing fake tan and bronzer, Rosie's all about being pale and interesting. Pared-down make-up (nude lips and lots of mascara for those huge blues) means she packs a punch when she up-styles with rouge lippy for an evening look. Relying heavily on black and nude palettes in her wardrobe and accessorising with chunky jewellery, as a style blogger she knows the best places to shop to get her fashion fix.

MY STYLE

PETER PILOTTO
'Elegant high-octane prints and colour.'
peterpilotto.com

AUSTIQUE
'Everything from fedoras to dresses, nail varnish to underwear.
austique.co.uk

THE SHOP AT BLUEBIRD
'A design-led boutique that stocks Phillip Lim and Peter Pilotto. It's heaven.'
theshopatbluebird.com

KAT MACONIE
'Sublime structured footwear that makes a statement.'
katmaconie.com

CÉLINE
'A Céline bag is probably my biggest extravagance – but they are investment pieces.'
celine.com

STYLE ICON
'Olivia Palermo has impeccable style, amazing hair and the cutest face. She's the dream.'

★ **MY TIP** ★

'Don't follow the tangerine
crowd. I hate fake tan.
When will people realise
there has never been
an orange person on
the cover of *Vogue*?
I love being pale and
I don't want to see your
orange hands!'

★ **MY TIP** ★

'Quality shoes and ties are essential. You could wear a suit that costs 50 quid, but if you've got a really nice tie and really good shoes, you'll still look the business.'

The City Boy
ANDY JORDAN

Andy's expressive nostrils cause more of a fuss than his style. But when it comes down to it, the cutesy trader is generally pretty well turned out in typical West London uniform: Ralph Lauren shirt/v-neck and Ralph jumper/jeans/flying jacket. A trader by day and ladies man by night, Andy's quick to ditch his workaday suits for an uber-relaxed look on his dates. Hoodies, checked shirts and a smile, and Andy Jordan's good to go.

MY STYLE

RALPH LAUREN
'My favourite brand by a mile. The classic purple-label suits are works of art.'
ralphlauren.co.uk

HERMÈS & FERRAGAMO
'The only places to buy ties. Beautiful, subtle and they never look cheap.'
hermes.com
ferragamo.com

CHURCH'S & LOAKE
'Classic, high-quality British footwear – a wardrobe staple.'
church-footwear.com
loake.co.uk

GROOMING

DRAKES
'It has a great vibe and it's the best place in Chelsea for a wet-shave.'
drakesgrooming.com

STYLE ICON

'Johnny Depp is the coolest man on the planet. It doesn't matter what he puts on because just by wearing it he makes it cool.'

The High-street Honey
LUCY WATSON

Lucy is always immaculately groomed. Never seen without a blow-dry and a slick of liquid eyeliner on her top lids to add extra bite to those infamous death stares, pint-sized Lucy likes to shop on the high street, and to change up her look; one minute she's in a biker and a beanie, the next a skintight leather dress and then it's on to a preppy sweater and jeans. Chameleon.

MY STYLE

ZARA
'The colour palettes are so vibrant and the detailing is so quirky.'
zara.com

ALL SAINTS
'For an urban look, and I really like their textured knitwear.'
allsaints.com

TIFFANY
'I'm not too out there with jewellery. Tiffany pieces are classy, elegant and timeless.'
tiffany.co.uk

AD HOC
'I bought a jumper with "Hate Me" written across it. That's what everyone was feeling about me at the time so I thought I'd just embrace it.'
adhoclondon.co.uk

STYLE ICON
'I love Mary-Kate and Ashley Olsen. They are so funky, boho and weird.'

'I don't understand why people wear real fur when you can buy faux. I think it's disgusting. My advice would be to look up some videos online, see where fur comes from and you won't want to wear it again.'

'Dress to suit your figure.
I spent years trying to be
trendy regardless of my
shape, but I've realised that
doesn't make you look good
or feel confident.'

The Chic Chick
LOUISE THOMPSON

Doe-eyed Louise is always well put together; she may be petite but she sure stands out in a crowd. Neither shy nor retiring when it comes to clothes, Louise loves statement necklines — bold neckpieces, bejewelled collars — and she wears them with ease. Her trademark swoosh of eyeliner is a constant while her hair and lipstick are used to transform her look to suit the occasion.

MY STYLE

BURBERRY
'Their coats are just classic pieces. A Burberry coat will always be my favourite.'
uk.burberry.com

LIBERTY
'From scarves to cute accessories, I love having a mooch around all the different departments.'
liberty.co.uk

ZARA
'I could literally wear anything in there at the moment. They have a lot of petite sizes which is perfect for someone small like me.'
zara.com

PAMPERING

BLISS WORLD
'I love the oxygen facial. I don't know how on earth it works but afterwards your skin feels totally revitalised.'
blissworld.co.uk

STYLE ICON
'Leighton Meester from Gossip Girl looks perfect in whatever she wears and she's fearless about trying new styles.'

The Fashionista
VICTORIA BAKER-HARBER

Victoria is at one with SW1. Designer, designer, designer — she wouldn't be seen dead in Sloane Square unless she was impeccably turned out. Her staples? Louboutins (she collects them), huge hair, kohl-rimmed eyes hidden beneath oversized shade and on her arm the latest must-have tote. Queen of the pithy put-down, swimsuit designer Victoria's style is an interesting combo: one part fashion-forward, one part Sloane, the occasional hint of (shock horror!) high street, but always a dash of Fijian va-va-voom.

MY STYLE

ALAÏA

'My absolute favourite for seamless dresses, and I love their shoes too. The craftsmanship never dates.'
alaia.fr

MARY KATRANTZOU

'A young Greek designer based in London. I adore her bold graphic prints.'
marykatrantzou.com

BALMAIN

'There's a stylish rock-chick glamour to Balmain. Their signature shoulder pads give you the perfect shape.'
balmain.com

ZARA

'I admit I love having a blow-out in Zara. High-street shopping can be so much fun!'
zara.com

STYLE ICON

'Olivia Palermo is never anything less than immaculate and her look is elegance personified.'

★ MY TIP ★

'People love talking about my hair for some reason and I swear by dry shampoo — I buy it by the truckload, so I'm probably keeping them in business. It lifts your hair like nothing else.'

The Classic Modern Gent
MARK FRANCIS VANDELLI

Flamboyant Mark Francis is always dripping in designer. Though he doesn't follow fashion trends per se, he has got serious amounts of style. Super-opinionated on his likes and dislikes, especially when it comes to the sartorial, this very modern gent is dapper in the extreme. Blazers, open-necked shirts and pocket squares coupled with slim pants, cashmere knee-high socks and loafers – always the best of the best. Mark Francis in Superdry, chinos and Nike Airs? Don't be ridiculous, darling.

MY STYLE
VALENTINO
'It's all about elegance. I love the designer – he's a friend and a wonderful man.'
valentino.com

SANTONI
'You can't beat traditional Italian craftsmanship.'
santonishoes.com

GROOMING
NEVILLE
'When I'm in London I have my hair cut here because they know exactly what I like.'
nevillehairandbeauty.net

STYLE ICON
'I believe Tom Ford is a man who typifies taste, elegance and self-awareness in a way that's not overt. He has an attention to detail that is key to everyday life.'

★ MY TIP ★
'Don't overdo it, never be too fashion-conscious and don't wear everything at once. That's not a look!'

★ *Mark Francis and Victoria dish the Chelsea fashion dos and don'ts on pages 82-86.*

ON TREND

Fabulous or faux pas? *Made in Chelsea's* formidable fashionistas Victoria and Mark Francis on their loves and loathes...

MENSWEAR

Mark Francis says: 'There's so much choice out there, it's very easy to get caught up in terrible looks. The biggest risk in terms of what you wear is to follow fashion too closely. Trying too hard to be in vogue is the worst fashion faux pas anyone can make. Mindlessly wearing what's on the catwalk demonstrates a complete lack of personality and real style. One has to have good taste to make a look work – most people need to be very careful.'

FABULOUS

FAUX PAS

ROCK THE CROC

MF: 'I'm a bit of a Russian oligarch at heart and I adore croc. My alligator shoe collection is out of control. I probably have about 40 pairs and they are all the same style. My tip for men's footwear is to have one style of shoe that you wear, and stick to it.'

WEAR YOUR CONFIDENCE

MF: 'You have to feel self-assured in what you are wearing – which means clothes that are appropriate to what you're doing, to your lifestyle and to your body shape.'

QUALITY IS KING

MF: 'The key to men's fashion is quality, cut and style. If you know you're wearing something that's well made and timeless, you know you can be confident in it. Elegance is fundamental in a man's wardrobe, so stick to classic styles and traditional fabrics. My look is not wash at 30 degrees; my look is dry clean only.'

LOOKING LIKE A SLOB

MF: 'I couldn't leave the house unless I was groomed and dressed correctly. It's not that I'm concerned about what other people think about me, it's what I think of myself. If you dress like a slob, you feel like a slob. I don't own a tracksuit, I have never worn a tracksuit and I would never do anything that would involve me wearing a tracksuit.'

DRESSING INAPPROPRIATELY

MF: 'For me, being somewhere and feeling inappropriately dressed is the most awful faux pas. You have to blend into your environment. If I'm travelling to the South of France, Venice or Capri, I know they are places for which I have a wardrobe. If I was to take a voyage to some unknown place, I'd have to get a new wardrobe to suit it, because there's nothing worse than looking out of place or uncomfortable.'

MEN AND MASCARA

MF: 'Don't get me started on men and make-up – let's not go there! Unless you are a movie star, then you just don't wear it. Ever. It's not a look!'

WOMENSWEAR

Victoria says: 'Money can't buy style. Even if you don't have the cash for designer, you can still look so much better than people with money but no taste. I see so many people in London who haven't got a clue how to put something together; they buy all the latest trends and wear a whole collection in one go. Not a good look! Don't wear what's in fashion regardless of what actually suits you. Truly stylish people are the ones who want to express themselves through their clothing.'

FABULOUS

FAUX PAS

EMBRACE COLOUR

V: 'Life's too short not to brighten your look. It lifts your mood and, if you can find your colour, it also lifts your face. Don't overdo it – wear colour on the top or bottom, but keep other pieces in complementary neutrals.'

CREATE A CAPSULE WARDROBE

V: 'A good, timeless, A-line dress will never go out of date, and a stock of plain black and white t-shirts is essential, as are a pair of killer heels. Create a core wardrobe of quality items, then experiment with more inexpensive, trend-driven accessories.'

KEEP WARM IN STYLE

V: 'Let your outer garments do the talking and invest in a bold statement coat for winter. It's a timeless, understated look – and very Chelsea!'

BEING A LABELS SNOB

V: 'Don't be a slave to designer. It doesn't matter where something is from or how much it costs. I could be wandering around a flea market in India and see something I love for 99p. So the rule is: forget about the label; if you like it, buy it!'

FLASHING THE FLESH

V: 'You'll never see me walking around with my boobs hanging out wearing some slutty little dress. High crotch-lines and shorts where your ass is bursting out make me want to reach for the sick bag too. Don't get everything out at once, dress for each season according to your body shape and always try and flatter your best assets.'

UGG-LY BOOTS

V: 'Why would any woman choose to wear Ugg boots in public? I can just about cope with the idea of putting them on to take the dog for a walk (in the middle of the night), but otherwise there's no excuse. They are unfeminine and flatter no one!'

Heaven scent?

★

*Putrid perfume is
Mark Francis's pet hate...*

'Wearing too much perfume is just ghastly. Before someone even enters the room you already know they are there, and that's not chic. I just want to go to the bathroom and wash it off them. You may be a nice person, but if you're wearing bad perfume, I dislike you before you've even opened your mouth. Your scent is your signature, it's something you carry with you all the time, so you must choose it carefully. Personally, I love amber, a hint of musk, vanilla and a touch of oud.'

★ ★ ★

"Don't wear what's in fashion regardless of what actually suits you."
VICTORIA

"Trying too hard to be in vogue is the worst fashion faux pas anyone can make."
MARK FRANCIS

CHELSEA
FITNESS

BODY BEAUTIFUL

★

Fancy being toned like Rosie or pumped like Proudlock?
Here's how they do it...

HULA-HOOPING

Watching a Lycra'd Ollie haplessly gyrating away whilst being interrogated about his love life by super-hooper Cheska was one of the funniest things ever, but there's no doubt hooping is a seriously effective workout. According to recent studies, hula-hooping can burn seven calories per minute while boosting energy levels, building stamina and increasing concentration. The use of a weighted hoop adds greater resistance, thereby strengthening and toning your abs more effectively. No wonder Beyonce is a fan.
hooping.org

"The pain is so worth the gain."
ROSIE

PILATES BOOT CAMP

This is no ordinary Pilates class… Prepare to be barked at drill-sergeant style as you get a core muscle resistance-based workout using state-of-the-art reformer machines. It's fierce but fun, and as well as giving you a leaner body, regular sessions can improve posture, breathing and concentration. Devotee Rosie says: 'The pain is so worth the gain!'
bootcamppilates.com

SQUASH

All four of the boys worked up a sweat, but it was Jamie and Spencer who surprised even themselves by thrashing sportier types Andy and Sam at this fast-moving and high-impact game. Squash provides an all-round cardiovascular workout and is a great way to let off steam. Playing regularly increases strength and also promotes good co-ordination, agility and flexibility.
stghltc.co.uk

DOG-WALKING

Taking her Cavalier King Charles Spaniel for walkies helps Binky keep trim. Having a dog to walk encourages daily exercise – Binky's on Wimbledon Common for an hour each morning with Scrumble. It will improve your cardiovascular fitness, decrease stress and your handbag-doggie will love you for it too!

BOOT CAMP

With a physique that yo-yos more than his love life, Spencer lost just under a stone in three days while attending the No 1 Boot Camp in Ibiza. Blaming his extra bulk on gorging as yet another relationship went pear-shaped, the hardcore regime included early-morning workouts, four-hour hikes and eight-hour training sessions led by ex-army instructors. Binky's also a fan, having shed a stone in a week at a Norfolk venue. She says: 'It's perfect for me because I like being outside and I get really bored in the gym. It was really full on, but I'm the sort of person who needs to be shouted at if you want me to do some exercise!'
no1bootcamp.com

RUNNING

Who else but cool-as-a-cucumber Proudlock could manage to successfully chat up a fellow sprinter whilst legging it around Battersea Park at running club. Clearly a run has the potential to give your heart muscle an effective workout in more ways than one.
runclub.co.uk

"I'm the sort of person who needs to be shouted at if you want me to do some exercise."
BINKY

DOGA

★

It's yoga for you – and your dog! The pooches get involved by acting as weights to help balance their owners or by doing some of the moves themselves. 'You meditate at the beginning and the dogs just run around. Then you're taught to pant like a dog so that they come to you. It's all about bonding with your dog while you work out,' explains Cheska. 'I'm sure the girls thought I was mad for making them do it, but at the end Millie's massive French Bulldog Herbie was completely relaxed and flopped on the floor.'

dogamahny.co.uk

TENNIS

It's not just about strawberries and cream – tennis is a great all-round workout that boosts aerobic fitness and improves your balance. Research shows that a good hour-long game of singles burns around 600 calories for men and 420 calories for women. The standard looked fairly evenly matched when Francis and Rosie took on Jamie and Millie at mixed doubles, but their eyes were most definitely on the post-match Pimm's rather than the prize.
gardenstennis-sw19.co.uk

HORSE RIDING

Following in Ashley and Cheska's clippity-cloppity horse shoes by exploring the open trails of Wimbledon Common, it's hard to believe you're only minutes from central London. The common has 16 miles of riding courses, including long stretches suitable for trots and canters, ensuring a thorough cardiovascular workout. Regular riding tones your legs and increases core muscle strength.
wvstables.com

BARRECORE

A combination of ballet, yoga and Pilates, this LA-born fitness fad has taken the King's Road by storm. Classes consist of a sequence of movements designed to stretch muscle groups while using a ballet barre. With practice you'll become leaner, stronger and more flexible. However, when Chelsea girls Louise, Binky, Rosie and Millie piled up, there was definitely more gossip being dished than any bodies being stretched!
barrecore.co.uk

NO SWEAT

How to look good while keeping fit...

★

Keep it tight; loose-fitting shorts
and tops may reveal a bit too
much during a downward dog.

★

Choose a quick-drying performance
fabric; a cotton t-shirt can become
wet and will stay that way.

★

Keep make-up to a minimum;
a sweaty gym face with make-up
sliding down it isn't a good look!

Here's

STEVIE JOHNSON

'I won the cup for best-behaved boy…
but behind the angelic facade I was
actually quite sneaky.'

My claim to fame… when I was at pre-prep school I won the cup
for best-behaved boy. My mum was very proud, but the older I got
the more corrupt I got. Behind the angelic facade I was actually quite
sneaky. Spencer was the year above me at school, and he was always
trying to corrupt the younger boys to go and do naughty stuff. We
did a school rugby tour together and he was very much the ringleader,
getting us all to sneak out to the pub.

My guilty pleasure is… cheesy pop music. Everyone says my music
tastes are the same as a 15-year-old girl. Whether it's One Direction or
Justin Bieber, I'm not afraid to put my hands in the air and sing along.

I'm a writer… when I was at school it was one of the few things
I was really good at, and I've got back into it recently. I find it a great
way to relax and take my mind off things. I'd love to write a play –
but I'm not sure I could top the real-life drama that happens on
the show!

Ed Sheeran sang on my coffee table… he stayed with me and Andy
at uni in Leeds because one of our housemates knew him from school.
This was before he'd made it and none of us really knew who he was.
But we invited some people round, had a few beers and he got up and
performed on our coffee table. He totally blew us away.

Here's

CHESKA HULL

'The girls at my school were known as "double cream" – rich and thick basically.'

My name used to be Chloe... I was born in Bangkok – because my parents worked there – and was named Chloe Francesca Hull. But no one in Thailand could say Chloe properly. They'd call me 'Shlooey' or 'Chilowe', so my parents swapped my names around and got me a new birth certificate.

Boarding school was the best time of my life... the author of *St Trinian's* allegedly based it on my school, which was a former convent, and we were very naughty indeed. One night we spray-painted 'We're no angels!' on the side of the gym, but we misspelt it so it actually read 'We're no *angles*!' They tried to scrub it off but didn't quite manage it and you can still see it faintly even now. The girls at my school were known as 'double cream' – rich and thick basically.

My inappropriate celebrity crush is... Simon Cowell. I hadn't given him a second thought until I had a dream where I was trying to get him to have sex with me. Then the next day I woke up and saw him on television and suddenly I fancied him in real life. I do find the power he wields to be very attractive.

I have a pretty foul party trick... it starts off with Binky making my nipple really cold by rubbing it with ice, then we balance CDs on it to see how many we can get to hang on my erect nipple before they fall off. The most we've done is five – although Binky is convinced we once managed six.

CHELSEA
PARDIES

PARTY PEOPLE

Partying is what the group does best, but
as ever there was plenty of awkwardness
behind the masks at Mark Francis's
glamorous masquerade ball...

Masked in mystery and draped in decadence, masquerade balls have been taking place since the 15th century, most enthusiastically in Venice as part of their Carnival celebrations. These parties became increasingly popular across Europe as an occasion where rich and poor could mingle in ways normally prohibited by the class divide – and now they're enjoying something of a renaissance in SW1!

They looked slightly bewildered when Mark Francis announced he was staging the event. 'Think Guy Bourdin, think silk gloves and Duchesse satin. It will be divine!' he declared, adding,

'Bring leopards!' But on the night everyone embraced the extravagant theme. As she slinked over to Lucy and Binky, Phoebe looked suitably Cruella de Vil in a sharp gothic ensemble with long black gloves and a sheer mesh mask. 'You've made it very clear you have no real interest in making friends with any of the girls,' accused Binky, sporting a sleek Venetian filigree mask dotted with Swarovski crystals. 'No, it's just you two...' pouted Phoebe, from behind her veil.

Make-up artist Millie did away with a traditional mask and opted for 'masquerade make-up' with oversized lacy eyebrows and

extravagant false lashes, while nice guy Josh showed his dark side by wearing a handcrafted *Phantom of the Opera*-style white leather mask.

Jamie was playful in black eyewear trimmed with an antique devil's face, but it was Francis who stood out amongst the boys in a traditional hand-painted Venetian long-nose mask. 'It's for the aristocrats to scare off the peasants,' he explained, but an amused Rosie (hidden behind an intricate lace filigree number) informed him he could do some serious damage with what could only be described as his slightly rude and phallic beak.

★ **What they ate**
Marinated Italian bocconcini canapés wrapped in Parma ham

★ **What they drank**
Prosecco Ca' degli Ermellini (Italy)

HOW TO THROW A MASKED BALL...

By invitation only; this is not the occasion for a blasé 'invite-all' via social media. Send your cards by post.

★

Get creative; keep it classic or opt for a theme such as black and white, fairy tales or angels and demons.

★

Set the stage; drapes, peacock feathers and safely positioned candelabras create a suitably opulent atmosphere.

★

The music of the night; hire a string quartet or create a playlist that includes dramatic Mozart or Beethoven. This is not the night for Rihanna.

IT'S MY PARTY

★

...and I'll cry if I want to! There's always a drama
at a Made in Chelsea *shindig.*

ANDY AND STEVIE'S PROHIBITION PARTY The gang made the
trip to (shock horror) NW6 for this 1920s-themed bash at Kilburn's Love
& Liquor DJ bar. The speakeasy-styled interior was perfect for Prohibition-
style partying, but it all ended in a slanging match between enemies
Jamie and Lucy over the rumours he'd been spreading about her.

MARK FRANCIS'S 'RIVIERA CHIC' PARTY Panicking that his
chosen 1950s glamour theme would result in clichéd attire, Mark
Francis announced: 'If anyone turns up dressed like Marilyn Monroe,
then I am going to heave!' Instead, the only faux pas at the Surrey
mansion party was Lucy and Spencer exchanging numbers behind
his girlfriend Louise's back. This resulted in a tumultuous showdown
between the couple and the inevitable Louise blub-fest.

BINKY'S BARN DANCE Everyone decamped to Berkshire for
Binky's country-style hoedown where Ollie faced a few home truths.
'You know I'm pretty much gay; the only person who doesn't know
is me,' he sighed to Binky and Cheska, only weeks before randomly
bedding Fran.

THE LOST BOIS NEVERLAND PARTY Proudlock, Francis and
Jamie's *Peter Pan*-themed birthday bash at The Roof Gardens in
Kensington was supposed to be an enchanting celebration of childhood
– but despite the fact that he'd rocked up in his pyjamas and was clutching
a teddy bear, Francis was so offhand with Sophia (because of her
dalliance with Proudlock) that she started to sob. Cue an incredibly
awkward silence between the pair of them.

THE PARTY RULES

The guide to leaving a party with your head held high...

★

Eat before you go out. Imbibing on an empty
stomach is a one-way ticket to social embarrassment.

★

Remember your manners. Compliment
the host on the party and their outfit
(whether you mean it or not).

★

Be socially aware and introduce yourself
to other guests if the host is preoccupied.

★

Punctuate alcohol consumption with a soft drink.
Tipsy and playful is fun; loud and boorish isn't.

★

Keep conversation light, bright and polite.
Crossing the line into controversy is a no-no.

★

Always thank the host before exiting. For more
formal events, email or send a thank-you note
within the week.

THOROUGHLY MELODRAMATIC MILLIE

She knows how to make a bash go with a bang...

CASINO PARTY

On discovering boyfriend Hugo had cheated, Millie got her revenge by throwing a perfectly good vodka martini in his face and dumping him. But perhaps most devastating of all – she blocked him on Twitter. Ouch.

FRANCIS AND MARK FRANCIS'S ROARING TWENTIES PARTY

Dressed as a flapper, Millie took to the mic to announce Hugo and Rosie's betrayal. 'A toast to my best friend Rosie for hooking up with Hugo Taylor when we were together and lying about it.' Cue audible gasps from the others. 'Here's to friendship!' she sneered, adding, 'You're disgusting' as she stormed past teary-eyed Rosie.

COUNTRY HOUSE PARTY

On hearing from Francis that Spencer had cheated on Louise, Millie and Rosie marched over to have it out with him. Louise shed some tears, but when an indignant Spencer tried to shout Millie down, she shut him up with a swift smack around the chops. Spenny was nearly as shell-shocked as his stinging cheek!

DINNER PARTYING

Staying in is the new going out and the sign of a good soirée is that everyone has had fun, including the host. All it takes is a little planning — follow these simple guidelines and you're guaranteed to be the hostess with the mostest...

SET THE SCENE

Flowers and candles are an easy way to create an atmosphere, but make sure they're below eye level so that you can see your guests. Avoid blooms with an overpowering scent.

GET IN THE MOOD

Select music to suit the atmosphere you want to create. Make a dinner party playlist – your background beats can also be a good conversation starter.

KNOW YOUR NIBBLES

Prepare canapés so that guests have something to munch on whilst waiting for the others to arrive. A bowl of cheesy Wotsits will not suffice.

KEEP IT SIMPLE

The object of the exercise is to have a good time, so choose a menu that doesn't involve you spending all night in the kitchen. Check with guests for any special dietary requirements and practise your dishes in advance. Look as if you haven't got a care in the world by choosing a starter and a dessert that can be prepared earlier in the day and a main that requires minimal faffing once everyone has arrived. If it's still stressing you out – cheat. That's what Marks & Spencer was invented for!

BE OUR GUEST

Fine-tune your guest list to ensure everyone has an enjoyable evening. Make sure there's a balanced mix of the sexes, that the invitees are socially flexible and that the group is compatible. For a truly relaxed evening, stick to those in your immediate circle.

PLAN THE SEATING

It's traditional to sit married couples apart, whilst engaged or courting couples should be positioned together. However, separating people who know each other to different sections of the table can help facilitate conversation.

KICK-START THE CHAT

A good trick is to inform your guests that the seating plan has been arranged based on things they have in common – everyone will immediately try to figure them out. When they've announced their findings, you can reveal it was all a ruse to get them chinwagging!

I'LL DRINK TO THAT

A cocktail on arrival is a great way to lubricate any initial social awkwardness, however the host should refrain from intoxication until the main is safely on the table. Make sure you pair your wine with the food and give each bottle the chance to breathe before serving.

GAME FOR A LAUGH

Having cleared the table, after-dinner games are a good way to keep the party going. 'I have never', 'Spin the bottle' and 'Who am I?' rarely fail. Camera-bombing (like pass-the-parcel but with a camera on timer and without the music) is another crowd-pleaser – just make sure you don't drop it in your coffee!

'There's nothing more depressing than going to a dinner party where there aren't any flowers. Doesn't it just kill you?'
MARK FRANCIS

'If your parents are there, you want a pretty girl who can charm your father and a well-mannered boy to sweet-talk your mother.'
VICTORIA

'You need a good wine cellar to have a dinner party – otherwise go to a restaurant!'
MARK FRANCIS

'The secret of a successful dinner party is a handful of good humoured characters and some darn good red wine.'
ROSIE

TABLE MANNERS

Wait until everyone else has been served and the host
has begun eating before picking up your cutlery.

★

Always taste food before adding salt and pepper.
Never ask for condiments unless they are
already on the table.

★

Never talk with your mouth full, even if you
have some huge gossip you're desperate to dish.

★

Wine glasses are held by the stem – pinch the
stem between your index finger and thumb.

★

Under no circumstances stretch across a fellow diner.
Ask for items to be passed along the table.

★

Learn from Lucy and Andy's faux pas at Rosie's
dinner party – it's *never* socially acceptable to eat
each other's faces at the dining table.

CHELSEA COCKTAILS

★

*They are mad for martini in SW1.
Here's how they shake it...*

PORN STAR MARTINI

Lucy's favourite tipple
is a glamorous and
contemporary classic.

INGREDIENTS

2 teaspoons vanilla sugar
50ml vanilla vodka
25ml passion fruit liqueur
10ml passion fruit purée
A shot of champers
Fresh passion fruit, to garnish

★ Shake all the ingredients
(except the champagne)
and strain into a martini glass.

★ Garnish withfresh passion
fruit if desired.

★ Serve the champers on
the side in a shot glass.

KETEL ONE DIRTY MARTINI

When it comes to cocktails,
Spencer likes his dry
and dirrrrty.

INGREDIENTS

50ml Ketel One vodka
2 tablespoons olive brine
1 tablespoon dry vermouth
1 whole green olive

★ Pour the vodka, brine and
vermouth with a handful of
ice into a cocktail shaker and
shake well.

★ Transfer to a martini
glass and add the olive.

ESPRESSO MARTINI

Andy gets a buzz from this sparky little pick-me-up.

INGREDIENTS

50ml vodka
25ml Galliano liqueur
25ml fresh espresso
1 teaspoon sugar syrup

★ Place all the ingredients into a cocktail shaker with a handful of ice and shake hard.

★ Strain into a martini glass. As an alternative, try vanilla-flavoured vodka.

AND FOR THE MORNING AFTER...

You can't beat a classic Bloody Mary to beat those hangover blues.

INGREDIENTS

50ml vodka
1 tablespoon freshly squeezed lemon juice
150ml tomato juice
6 dashes Worcestershire sauce
3 dashes Tabasco sauce
Pinch of salt and freshly ground pepper
Celery stick

★ Pour the vodka (plus a couple of ice cubes) into a tall glass, followed by the lemon juice, tomato juice and sauces.

★ Adjust the seasoning to taste and add a celery stick to serve.

Here's

PHOEBE-LETTICE THOMPSON

'I was completely obsessed with *Vogue* and my bedroom walls were covered in magazine cut-outs.'

***I loved athletics*…** my events at school were the 100 and 200 metres and the long jump. I was fearless. I think if I had to do a long jump now I'd be a lot more scared than I was then. I remember once a girl competing before me snapped the bone in her leg in half as she jumped. It didn't faze me at all, but I'm sure if I saw that now I'd be quite repulsed.

***My weakness is*…** antique jewellery. My father is an antique jewellery dealer, so I've grown up with it and I know what I like – which is usually expensive! I've got a ring that says Phoebe on it that my father got for me before I was born. I love it because it's Victorian and it has my name on it – which shows how old my name is, doesn't it?

***I've subscribed to* Vogue *since I was 13*…** it's a cliché but fashion is my passion and it was always the field I wanted to end up in. I was completely obsessed with *Vogue* and my bedroom walls were covered in magazine cut-outs and photography. I was fascinated by it all, so I interned at a couture house when I was 16 and now I work at *Tatler*. It's my dream.

***My favourite film is*…** Baz Luhrmann's *Romeo and Juliet*. Everything about that film makes me want go there. I wouldn't want to be Juliet because we all know what happened to her, but I'd love to be Romeo's friend or someone like that. I just want to live in that world.

Here's

OLIVER PROUDLOCK

'I was on a bursary, so I had to
be careful, otherwise… I could've
been chucked out.'

I've worn earrings since I was 15… I used to wear a guitar string
in my ears to keep the holes open because earrings weren't allowed at
Eton. Potentially they could've looked quite cool with my tailcoat, but
I didn't want to get into any trouble. I was on a bursary, so I had to be
quite careful, otherwise they might have taken it away and I could've
been chucked out.

I get my creative side from my mum, Lena… Mum's a
photographer, a designer and she used to have her own clothes
line in the 70s. Ever since I was a really young kid a lot of it came
from her. I was lucky in the sense that my parents were always really
supportive with me doing art and eventually specialising in it. When
I went to school, the facilities we had were amazing and I'd spend
every day in the art department. That's where I developed my love
for design, which I have now developed into a career.

My proudest achievement is… getting my fashion label Serge
DeNimes into Harrods. I studied Fine Art at Newcastle University
where I used to put my art on t-shirts and it just grew from there.
We always went to Harrods when I was a kid, so to see my clothes
in there was a pretty big moment for me.

My mum is the show's number-one fan… she has appeared
a couple of times and totally loved it. Like a bit too much. She's
obsessed with *Made in Chelsea* and is always pestering me about
how she could be in it on a more regular basis. I think she wants
to be on it full-time. I'm like, Mum, I'm not so sure…

A GUIDE
TO THE
SEASON

Back in the 18th century the social season marked the time of year when society families left their country estates and headed to Mayfair. There, girls would be presented to the monarch before embarking on a whirlwind of parties, balls and prestigious occasions such as Royal Ascot. The bit about country estates and being introduced to royalty may have changed (unless you bump into them stumbling out of Mahiki), but otherwise the modern season remains a partying paradise, combining glamorous sporting events with hedonistic international jaunts. From polo in Windsor to pool parties in Ibiza, here's your guide to the must-do social calendar...

SPRING

A GUIDE TO THE SEASON

PLACES TO BE SEEN

And how to do it in style

THE BOAT RACE

★

Since 1836 the contest has taken place annually on a stretch of the Thames in south west London between Putney and Mortlake, where thousands of spectators descend on the riverbanks to soak up the atmosphere.

This uniquely British row-off between Oxford and Cambridge Universities began in Henley-on-Thames in 1829 as a challenge between two old school chums. The race (held at the end of March or beginning of April) can be watched from either side of the river, but the prime viewing spots are to be found by Putney Bridge, from the towpath along Putney Embankment (get there early to bag your spot),

and at the finish, just before Chiswick Bridge. The record time for the four-and-a-quarter-mile course is 16 minutes 19 seconds, which was set by Cambridge in 1998. If you couldn't give a monkeys who wins but like the idea of getting tipsy while ogling muscled young bucks thrusting away in the water, get yourself down to the pubs that line the route for some liquid refreshment. *theboatrace.org*

DRINK

THE BLUE ANCHOR
13 Lower Mall,
W6 9DJ
Traditional and
popular boat-race
venue – perfect for
riverside spectating.
blueanchorlondon.com

THE DOVE
19 Upper Mall,
W6 9TA
The oldest-
surviving riverside
pub in London has
a superb terrace.
dovehammersmith.co.uk

THE SHIP
10 Thames Bank,
Ship Lane, SW14 7QR
This cheery
Victorian watering
hole is practically on
the finish line.
taylor-walker.co.uk

CANNES FILM FESTIVAL

★

*All year round, Cannes is one of the chicest towns on
the Côte d'Azur — but it really comes alive in May.*

Film stars and filmmakers descend for the famous industry festival, turning this small seaside resort into one big red-carpeted party. It's the most prominent film festival in the world and has been going strong for more than 60 years. Thousands of flicks are screened over the two-week period, with some tickets available to the public. As evening falls, the open-air Cinéma de la Plage screens Cannes classics and out-of-competition films on the magical Plage Macé.
festival-cannes.fr

★ ★ ★ ★ ★

STAY
Hôtel du Cap-Eden-Roc
This château-like hotel is a Cannes institution. Demand a desirable room with a sea view over the Med.
hotel-du-cap-eden-roc.com

PARTY
Le Bâoli
The place to find Cannes' party elite. This lavish lounge club boasts tented cabanas where the international jet set can go wild in private.
lebaoli.com

" It's an absolute circus but it's terribly glamorous; a world-class grouping of fabulous people. "
MARK FRANCIS

MONACO GRAND PRIX

★

Billionaires, rock stars and supermodels all flock to Monte Carlo, leaving no doubt that this Grand Prix is the most glamorous of them all.

The inaugural race on the party town's famous street circuit took place in 1929 and was won by Brit William Grover-Williams in a dark green Bugatti – as a result, the colour became known as 'British Racing Green'. Run on an annual basis (in late May) since 1955, the Monaco Grand Prix has become the most prestigious racing event on the planet. Watch from the many grandstands erected around the 78-lap circuit – with a bottle of bubbly, of course!

grand-prix-monaco.com

★ ★ ★ ★ ★

STAY
The Monte-Carlo Beach
Combining the spirit of the Riviera's golden age with the vibe of a modern luxury resort, it also boasts an Olympic-sized swimming pool.
monte-carlo-beach.com

SHOP
Victoria loves to bag her Diors, Guccis and Pradas at Monte Carlo's Cercle d'Or. You'll find your Cartiers, Van Cleefs and Bulgaris in the Place du Casino.

GETTING AWAY

When springtime in Chelsea becomes
too much, it's time to escape...

AMSTERDAM

★

A bite-sized city with a big nightlife.

When the Chelsea posse landed, Ollie and Gabriella looked awkward on a tandem until Jamie turned up unannounced and apologised to Binky for being a prize chump. Far more exciting were Ollie and Gabriella's revelations the next day over breakfast – the exes had been flirting for weeks and finally they'd got it on. Twice!

★★★★

PARTY
Suzy Wong & Jimmy Woo
Sip a lychee Bellini at Suzy Wong's cocktail bar, then head across to its luxurious sister-nightclub, Jimmy Woo.
suzy-wong.nl
jimmywoo.nl

STAY
The Dylan
Amsterdam's most stylish boutique hotel. Located canal-side in the heart of the Nine Streets independent shopping district.
dylanamsterdam.com

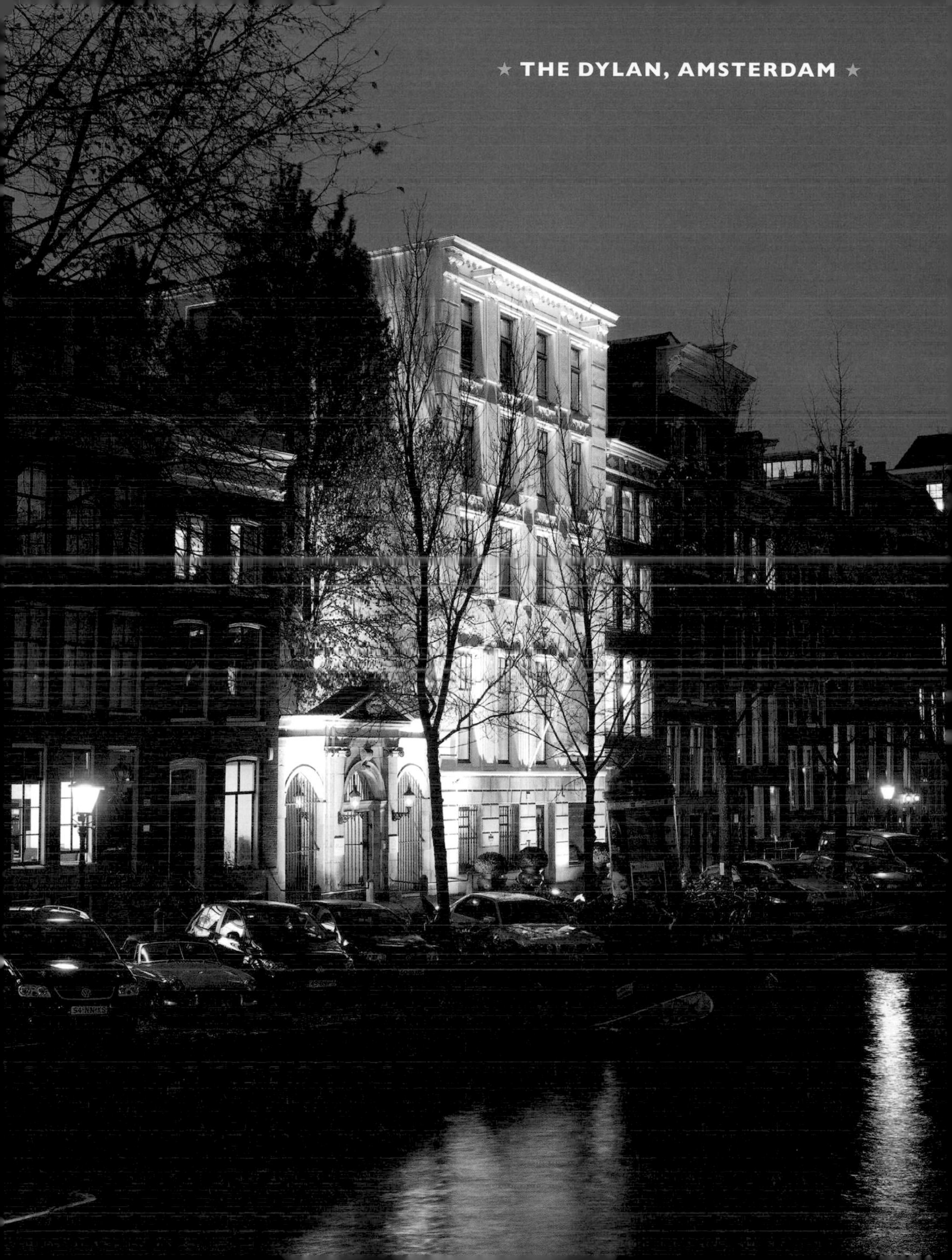

PARIS

★

*Where better for a romantic first date than
a stroll along the banks of the Seine.*

It was smug smiles all round when Spencer surprised Lucy with a trip to his favourite restaurant – which just happened to be in Paris! A chance for Spenny to show off his public schoolboy language (and French kissing) skills?

★★★★

EAT

La Tour d'Argent
This culinary institution is perfect for a romantic *tête-à-tête*. You can gaze dreamily at each other while taking in the breathtaking views across the Notre Dame.
latourdargent.com

STAY

Relais Christine
Set on a quiet side street in upmarket Saint Germain-des-Prés. Ask for a suite with French doors opening onto the private rear garden.
relais-christine.com

SALCOMBE

★

Dubbed Chelsea-on-Sea, this picturesque South Devon holiday spot is a sailing town with a villagey feel.

Surrounded by beautiful coves and with a seafront of picture-postcard houses curving around a bay, it's probably no surprise that Salcombe is a recent new entry on a list of UK millionaire hotspots, thanks to the number of Chelsea-ites buying second homes there.

★ ★ ★ ★ ★

SHOP
Amelia's Attic
This cute boutique stocks everything a girl could want, from bikinis to boots, jewellery to clutch-bags. It's also owned by Cheska's Mum.
ameliasattic.co.uk

STAY
South Sands Hotel
Boutique hotel with a preppie-meets-seaside vibe. The panoramic sea views across the horseshoe-shaped bay are to die for.
southsands.com

Here's

ANDY JORDAN

'I'll quite happily take all my clothes off
and jump in without a second thought.'

***I was a mischievous little boy*...** and I loved a good prank, which
I'd plan like a military operation. One night we broke into the main
teaching building at school, filled 900 cups of water and placed them
upside down all the way up the main stairwell. We then took around
seven kilometres of string and webbed the whole building so that no
one could get in to teach the next day. That didn't go down well at all.

***Surfing is my passion*...** Bali, Australia, New Zealand, Mexico,
Costa Rica, I've surfed in some awesome locations. I've actually nearly
drowned a few times as well and there are moments when you do think,
'Why am I doing this?', especially in the UK because it is just so cold.
Here I wear a wetsuit, boots, gloves and a hat that covers my entire
face. I look like a condom. A human condom.

***I'm very proud of my nostrils*...** people always ask me, 'Can you
flare your nostrils?' and I'm like, 'I dunno. Make me angry.' But I don't
mind it and I enjoy taking the mickey out of myself. They now have
their own Twitter account with over 12,000 followers, so they obviously
have a charm. Maybe my nostrils could get their own spin-off series?

***I love skinny dipping*...** whether it's in the Caribbean or someone's
swimming pool, I'll quite happily take all my clothes off and jump in
the water without a second thought. I did a photo shoot about skinny
dipping recently and had my photo taken at an outdoor lido in North
London. It was perhaps the coldest I have ever been, and thanks to
the shrinkage I'm sure that's the worst I have ever looked naked.

Here's

LOUISE THOMPSON

'I cry all the time on the show and I don't know why – I'm actually a really smiley person.'

I was suspended from school... for being caught in my room with a boy. I got sent home but my parents were away, so they had to arrange for a babysitter to come and stay with me for a week. She was really strict but I still managed to sneak my boyfriend in without her noticing. I did get good grades at school but there was this group of us that wreaked havoc wherever we went. Hiding rotten fruit under people's mattresses and generally making teachers cry by being vile to them – we were such hideous bitchy schoolgirls.

My guilty pleasure is... Scotch eggs. They are the best food in the whole wide world. If I see one I have to buy it and I could happily eat 20 large ones in a day, given half the chance. I'm the same with pork pies, although I probably couldn't eat quite as many in one go.

The biggest misconception about me is... that I'm a cry baby. I seem to cry all the time on the show and I don't know why. I'm actually a really smiley happy-go-lucky person and it's unusual for anyone to see me sobbing my eyes out.

I want to bang my drum... I've been around a lot of musically talented people recently which has kind of inspired me to learn to play the drums. I've got Grade Eight on the piano but I wanted to do something completely different. So I bought myself a Yamaha drum kit – I'd love to rock out in front of an audience like Tré Cool from Green Day.

SUMMER

A GUIDE TO THE SEASON

PLACES TO BE SEEN
And how to do it in style

POLO
★

Polo is like hockey on horseback — but faster, more dangerous and with a much glitzier crowd!

Divided into short six-minute segments known as 'chukkas', the game was first played in Persia in 600 BC and became the chosen sport of the nobility in the 1850s. In the UK, high-ranking player Prince Philip helped form the Household Brigade Polo Club at Smith's Lawn in Windsor, Prince Charles has represented his country and Princes William and Harry are fans of the game. Highlights of the polo season include the Prince of Wales Trophy at the Royal County of Berkshire Polo Club in Windsor (late May) and the glamorous Cartier International Day at the Guards Polo Club in July.

The 'Divot Stomp' is the most widely known polo tradition; during half-time spectators are invited onto the field to socialise and ceremoniously stomp down the turf that has been beaten up by the horses' hooves. *hpa-polo.co.uk*

★ ★ ★ ★ ★

DRESS CODE
Smart casual. These are outdoor events, so dress appropriately for the weather. Think very carefully about shoes; if you're walking on grass, stilettos are a no-no!

144

WIMBLEDON

★

It's the longest-running and most prestigious tennis tournament on the planet.

The world of tennis descends on Wimbledon in south west London for two weeks every summer. The first Wimbledon was staged in 1877 by The All England Lawn Tennis & Croquet Club to raise money for a new roller and it wasn't until seven years later that the Ladies' Singles and Men's Doubles events were introduced.

There's a public ballot for tickets that closes in December and the event begins at the end of June. However, Wimbledon remains the only Grand Slam where fans can queue for tickets on the day for the show courts – although you may need to put up a tent the night before to guarantee yourself success! *wimbledon.com*

"I love Wimbledon more than anything. Drinking Pimm's and watching sport – you can't beat it." JAMIE

ROYAL ASCOT

★

The fashion highlight of the flat-racing calendar.

It was Queen Anne who first came up with the idea of a racecourse at Ascot while out riding in 1711. The first-ever race meeting took place that year and what is now known as Royal Ascot started to take shape with the Gold Cup in 1807, which is now the course's oldest-surviving race. The Queen has attended every day of Royal Ascot (held in June) since 1945 and she never looks happier than when cheering on one of her own nags past the winning post. *ascot.co.uk*

"I love the thrill of gambling on a horse... but I love winning even more!" **LOUISE**

★ ★ ★ ★

DRESS CODE
It's a potential minefield! For general admission smart attire must be observed; in the Royal Enclosure women are expected to wear formal day dress (dresses and skirts must be no more than two inches above the knee) and a hat. Off-the-shoulder or strapless dresses are not allowed. Men are required to wear morning dress (including a waistcoat) and a top hat. Check the website for the finer details.

GLORIOUS GOODWOOD

★

This five-day festival of flat racing has taken place on the Sussex Downs at the end of July since 1802.

King Edward VII called it 'a garden party with racing tacked on', and indeed with traditional bands playing, car-park picnics and bucket-loads of Pimm's, the whole event has a typically English feel. In 2012 the world's top-rated racehorse, Frankel, demolished the field, but when the *Made in Chelsea* gang hit the course, poor Jamie wasn't quite so lucky with his mare Candy Kitten – it ended up being a non-runner!
goodwood.co.uk

★★★★★

DRESS CODE
Stylish yet relaxed. Chic summer fashions are the vibe and hats are encouraged, while men are required to wear jackets and ties. For the traditional chap, linen suits and the classic 'Goodwood' Panama hat can be worn.

HENLEY ROYAL REGATTA

⭐

For five days in July, this small South Oxfordshire town becomes the hot ticket for rowing fanatics from across the globe.

The regatta has been held annually since 1839, except during the two World Wars. Originally mounted by the Mayor and people of Henley as a public attraction with a fair and other amusements, the emphasis rapidly changed so that competitive amateur rowing became its main purpose. The most prestigious race is The Grand Challenge Cup for Men's Eights (on a course of exactly one mile and 550 yards), which has been awarded since the regatta was first staged.
hrr.co.uk

★ ★ ★ ★ ★

DRESS CODE
Demure floral dresses and men in smart, often brightly coloured suits or rowing blazers and chinos. In the more formal Stewards Enclosure, women are not permitted to wear trousers and must ensure their hemline is below the knee. Hat wearing is not obligatory, although it is the norm.

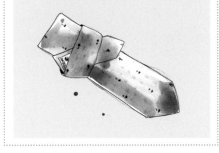

COWES WEEK

★

The largest sailing regatta of its kind in the world.

Held on the Isle of Wight, the first Cowes race took place in 1826 with just seven yachts – it now stages up to 40 daily races for around 1,000 boats over one week in early August and is the largest sailing regatta of its kind in the world. The 8,500 competitors range from Olympic and world-class professionals to weekend sailors. Away from the water the event has long been a magnet for the rich and famous and there's a laidback open-air party atmosphere – Chelsea favourites Mahiki and Raffles have recently opened pop-up outposts there. The event culminates on the Saturday with the prize-giving ceremony and a fabulous firework display.
aamcowesweek.co.uk

GETTING AWAY

Another soggy British summer?
It's time to seek out the sun…

THE HAMPTONS

★

*Pretend you're one of the Upper East Side elite and hit the social
scene whilst flashing plenty of pouty stares in this wealthy US enclave.*

The Hamptons (a series of small villages that dot the southern shore of Long Island) have long been the coastal destination of New Yorkers seeking respite from the summer heat of the city. The social events reach a peak on Labor Day weekend (the first Monday in September) when party people rub shoulders with celebrities, politicians and high-powered business types on the beaches and in the bars.

> "Anyone who's anyone wants a table at Nick and Toni's." **ANDY**

EAT

Nick & Toni's
The hottest restaurant in
East Hampton – this much-
loved eatery has a Tuscan vibe.
nickandtonis.com

STAY

The Montauk Beach House
Lively hotel where the
'Hampsters', i.e., hipsters (get
it?), hang out. Get ready for pool
parties and fashion shows galore.
thembh.com

IBIZA

★

*There's only one place for pure hedonism all
summer long – and it isn't Chelsea!*

The most bohemian Balearic island is a popular destination for the likes of Olivia, Fran and Millie. From long lazy lunches to the hottest pool parties, to the best clubbing in Europe, it's where the beautiful people come out to play!

★★★★★

PARTY
Blue Marlin
One of the island's coolest beach clubs, frequented by the likes of Kate Moss, Leonardo DiCaprio ... and Chelsea's very own Jamie Laing!
bluemarlinibiza.com

STAY
Ushuaïa Beach Hotel
Party-paradise beachfront hotel. There's also a surf-style restaurant and a chill-out minimalist spa.
ushuaiabeachhotel.com

ST TROPEZ

★

For decades it has been the French Riviera's
go-to destination for the rich and famous.

St. Tropez oozes cosmopolitan chic and Provençal charm in equal amounts. Hollywood starlets were going topless on the beach at a time it when would've been shocking anywhere else – there's always been something daring about this deceptively picturesque little town, with its pretty waterfront and bay full of bobbing yachts.

★ ★ ★ ★ ★

EAT
Le Club 55
Situated on Pampelonne Beach, the club has a private beachfront and an all-day restaurant where you could find yourself sitting next to Paris Hilton, Bono or even SW1 fashionista Victoria!
club55.fr

STAY
Pastis Hotel St Tropez
Eclectically decorated rooms set in a classically Provençal villa with private gardens lined with palm trees.
pastis-st-tropez.com

"I once spent £3,500 on a night out in St Tropez...it was so much fun it was almost worth it!" JAMIE

Here's

MILLIE MACKINTOSH

'I went to five different schools – I was determined to be as naughty as possible.'

I hacked off my little sister's hair... I went for her with a pair of kitchen scissors the day before we were due to be bridesmaids. I was only six years old and I don't even know why I did it. Luckily we had to wear these floral headbands for the wedding, which managed to hide the worst of it. I definitely got a smacked bottom that day.

I was a little devil at school... I went to five different schools because I was really rebellious and I was just determined to be as naughty as possible. Girls' boarding schools really are like St Trinian's. I remember the older girls once went to the lacrosse pitch in the middle of the night with some bleach and drew a huge penis on the grass.

I've always been a clothes horse... my sister Alice would put on a lot of Disney princess costumes, but I'd go straight for my mum's old clothes – some really great 80s Versace flame prints, miniskirts and heels that were way too big. I loved playing dress-up, but Alice's favourite game was riding the rocking horse. One time she put the bridle in my mouth, put the saddle on me and rode me round the house – pulling out a couple of my teeth in the process!

The biggest misconception about me... is that everyone refers to me as the Quality Street heiress. My great-great-great grandpa, John Mackintosh, did invent Quality Street, which I am really proud of, but my family don't own the company any more. I love all the old antique Mackintosh tins – we've got a huge collection of them on display in the kitchen. My favourite Quality Street? It has got to be the purple one.

Here's

SPENCER MATTHEWS

'I always cry when Mufasa dies in
The Lion King. I just can't handle it.'

I was a terrible student... one of my school reports read:
'Although I have done famous battle with this boy over the years,
the one truly irritating fact is that he openly boasts about getting
by without having done a thing.' I was shocking in the classroom,
but much more at home on the rugby field. There's this underlying
mockery of Etonians as pompous posh boys wandering around in
tailcoats sipping tea – but as it happens, we weren't too bad at sport.

I stuck porn to the ceiling of the cafeteria... we were always
sneaking out of our boarding house at night getting up to mischief,
but there was security around the school, so you had to be careful;
it was proper Jason Bourne stuff. One night we climbed onto the glass
roof of the cafeteria with a load of porn and superglued it face down
onto the glass. The next day the boys had a nice surprise over their
heads at breakfast, while the teachers were horrified. It was epic!

My celebrity crush... Princess Jasmine from *Aladdin*. She's the
perfect woman. I watch a lot of Disney films and whenever one
of my little nieces is round I'll slap on *Cinderella* or *Hercules* and
use them as an excuse to watch it. I always cry when Mufasa dies
in *The Lion King.* I just can't handle it.

I impersonate the **Made in Chelsea** *cast*... I do a good Millie –
you have to change the shape of your mouth, kind of purse your lips
together like a fish for it to sound right. I've done it in front of her and
we shared a smile, which is more than we have in the last ten years.

AUTUMN

A GUIDE TO THE SEASON

PLACES TO BE SEEN
And how to do it in style

THE CHELTENHAM OPEN
★

The Cheltenham three-day Open takes place in mid-November and is a major highlight of the British horse-racing calendar.

It begins with the ever-popular Countryside Day, which has a unique country fair atmosphere and a range of events such as hound parades, falconry displays and the season's first cross-country steeplechase. You won't go hungry either – there's a seemingly endless number of stalls and restaurants selling scrummy locally sourced produce. Tuck in!
cheltenham.co.uk

★ ★ ★ ★ ★

DRESS CODE
There is no dress code at Cheltenham. Racing takes place during the fresher months, so dress accordingly and wrap up warm.

CLAY PIGEON SHOOTING

★

Clay pigeon shooting is the art of firing at special flying targets,
known as clay pigeons, with a shotgun.

The terminology relates to times past when live pigeon-shooting competitions were held. Although these events were made illegal in 1921, a clay is still called a 'target', a hit is referred to as a 'hit' and the machine which projects the targets is known as a 'trap'. When the gang tried their hands at this country pursuit, there were raised eyebrows as well as raised rifles when Spencer and Funda rolled up. 'Who invited them?' sniffed Caggy. Relationship rivalry and guns = not a healthy combination! *cpsa.co.uk*

★ ★ ★ ★ ★

DRESS CODE
Blend in with the environment – you need to sport tweeds, greens and browns. Sturdy footwear is also required.

GETTING AWAY

You can't beat a change of scenery
to lift your autumnal mood...

LEWES

★

The Lewes Bonfire Night celebrations are the biggest in Britain.

Tens of thousands line the streets in this East Sussex market town to watch the fiery procession that traces its roots to 1605 when, during the reign of James I, Guy Fawkes and his fellow conspirators hatched the Gunpowder Plot in an attempt to blow up the Houses of Parliament and assassinate the king. The Lewes festivities culminate in five separate bonfire displays in which eerie effigies are destroyed by flames.
lewes.co.uk/Bonfire

★ ★ ★ ★ ★

STAY
Pelham House
Beautifully restored 16th century townhouse in the heart of Lewes with distant views of the South Downs.
pelhamhouse.com

EAT
Limetree Kitchen
Locally sourced seasonal produce are the ingredients for this eatery's classic European dishes.
limetreekitchen.co.uk

NEW YORK

★

You can't beat the golden glow of autumn in Central Park.

With its blue skies and crisp air, this is the perfect time to go walkabout in the city that never sleeps. Another great route is via the one-mile High Line, New York's aerial park created from an abandoned 1930s elevated railway in the Meatpacking District. You can stop off at the area's many restaurants, design studios and fashion boutiques along the way.

★ ★ ★ ★ ★

STAY
Crosby Street Hotel
Contemporary boutique hotel on a quiet cobbled street in the heart of vibrant SoHo.
firmdalehotels.com

DRINK
Jimmy
SoHo cocktail bar with a stylish 1970s vibe located 18 storeys above The James Hotel. Stunning panoramic views from the roof deck.
jimmysoho.com

"New York has a buzz like no other city in the world." VICTORIA

BARCELONA

★

Unlike the **Made in Chelsea** *crew's weekend at Spencer's rented villa, a trip to Barcelona doesn't have to involve poolside awkwardness!*

Every year towards the end of September the city holds its largest street party, the five-day Barcelona La Mercè Festival, in honour of La Mare de Déu de la Mercè, the Patron Saint of Barcelona. Some 600 events take place, including the not to be missed Correfoc (fire run), which involves 'devils' and other fire-spewing creatures.

★ ★ ★ ★ ★

STAY

Ohla Hotel
Central boutique hotel with roof deck and glass-sided swimming pool – the Correfoc practically passes its doors.
ohlahotel.com

EAT

Maitea
Eat like a local at this friendly tavern-like tapas bar which offers an excellent selection of generous-sized *pintxos* (smaller tapas on a toothpick).
maitea.es

Here's

LUCY WATSON

'The biggest misconception about me is that I'm a slut – I'm one of the least slutty people I know.'

I grew up on a farm... I was obsessed with the animals and I'd get up at 6 a.m. to feed the ducks and chickens. I delivered lambs too, so when I was six years old I became a vegetarian and I have been one ever since. I was a bit of a tomboy back then as well; I had really short hair and I'd wear dungarees and just run around in the mud all day.

I reached Grade Six in singing... I think you can teach with that qualification, so it's actually quite advanced. But then a little boy on a plane told me I was bad at singing when I was humming along to my iPod once and that just totally knocked my confidence. I never sang in public ever again.

The biggest misconception about me is... that I'm a slut, which is funny because I'm probably one of the least slutty people I know. I get a lot of people saying that I've slept with the whole of Chelsea, but I think if they knew how many people in Chelsea I'd actually slept with they'd be shocked – because up until a few months ago it was zero.

I always knew this was going to happen... it sounds weird and a bit arrogant, but I always knew I'd end up in the public eye. I'd been quite attention-seeking as a child and as a person in general, and everyone I know said I was the one most likely to succeed in this field. I think people are intimidated by me, so it takes someone quite gutsy to come and say 'hi' in the street. I suppose because on the show I come across as quite fiery and blunt, people are probably worried I'm going to turn on them!

Here's

OLLIE LOCKE

'If I could play any Shakespeare character it would be Orsino – he's such a f*cking drama queen!'

I'm a luvvie*…* I spent a year at RADA training to be an actor and really got stuck into my Shakespeare. If I could play any Shakespeare character it would have to be Orsino in *Twelfth Night* – he's such a f*cking drama queen. I auditioned to be Will in *The Inbetweeners*, but it was only when I saw the show that I understood why I hadn't got the part. I don't look anything like him.

My celebrity crushes are*…* Joanna Lumley and Denise Van Outen. Joanna is the perfect woman. She's the dream. I met her once and she said, 'When you make all your money darling … give it away', which I thought was an amazing thing to say. I've met Denise a few times too and I wrote about my obsession with her in my book. I used to sign RDA – Respect Denise Always – after my name every single time I wrote it.

I'm a night owl*…* I've worked in nine different clubs, on the door and looking after celebrities and years ago, clearing up. Actually, that was the best job I've ever had – it taught me some lessons that I'd never have learned through other things.

My guilty pleasure is*…* cheese and wine in bed. You can't beat it. I'm quite good with the crumbs and I make sure they don't fall into any nooks and crannies.

WINTER

A GUIDE TO THE SEASON

PLACES TO BE SEEN
And how to do it in style

SIX NATIONS CHAMPIONSHIP

★

The Six Nations is a hugely popular event held, handily for Chelsea types, in Twickenham, south west London.

It is the perfect occasion for novice spectators to join in with the good-natured crowd and cheer on beefy blokes in shorts as they tussle for glory. The origins of the Six Nations Championship date back to 1871, when teams from England and Scotland played in the first-ever Rugby Union international match.

Nowadays the tournament kicks off in February and the competing nations consist of England, Scotland, Ireland, Wales, France and Italy. On the final weekend the highly coveted Championship Trophy is presented to the victors; meanwhile, the losers have to make do with the symbolic wooden spoon! *rbs6nations.com*

POINT-TO-POINT

★

*'What's the point of a Point-to-Point?' Point-to-Point racing
is essentially steeplechase racing for amateur riders.*

The above queston was asked by a bemused Ollie as the gang turned up at the Horseheath races in Cambridgeshire – but after a few glugs of champagne he soon got into the swing of it. The origins of the sport can be traced back to riders racing their hunting horses from one church steeple to another over natural countryside and jumping whatever obstacles crossed their path along the way.

> **"Chelsea types like to get their wellies on and drink champagne in a field."** CHESKA

There are now over 200 fixtures across the country each season (which runs from the end of November until the following June), and with your picnic and a crate of booze packed into the boot of your car, it makes for the perfect day out in the country. *pointtopoint.co.uk*

★★★★★

DRESS CODE
There is no dress code as such, but think tweedy country casuals. Wellies and a warm coat are also a good way to battle the elements during winter fixtures.

GETTING AWAY

Brrrrr! Here are your emergency
winter-sun destinations...

DUBAI

★

Maze-like souks and giant shopping palaces.

Dubai is the ultimate destination if you fancy sun-kissed beaches combined with retail therapy. The Mall of the Emirates is so vast it even has its own indoor ski slope! Everyone jetted to the Emirates for Louise's birthday and the heat added to the sexual tension when Spencer decided he didn't want Sophie (the date he'd flown out with) and jumped into bed with his ex, Louise, instead. If you want to really escape from it all, just do a Francis – wrap yourself in a traditional headscarf and disappear into the desert on horseback.

★★★★

STAY
Raffles Dubai
Luxurious hotel in its own botanical gardens, positioned close to the magnificent Khan Murjan souk.
raffles.com

EAT
Atlantis The Palm
The iconic Atlantis The Palm has everything from its own outpost of Nobu to underwater eatery Ossiano, awarded 'Best Seafood Restaurant 2013' by *Time Out Dubai*.
atlantisthepalm.com

ATLANTIS THE PALM, DUBAI

"I was recognised in Dubai by a group of Iranian girls... *Made in Chelsea* must be on everywhere." FRANCIS

★ ★ ★ ★ ★

EDEN ROCK – ST BARTHS ★

ST BARTHS

★

It's clear why A-listers flock to St Barths (Saint Barthélemy)
in the French West Indies.

The island may be little more than eight square miles, but its surrounded by pink and white coral sand beaches, tiny coves and a lush tropical interior that's divine. What's not to like when you can chill on an isolated shore or dine on barbecued fish plucked straight from the Caribbean sea. It certainly beats south west London!

★ ★ ★ ★ ★

STAY

Eden Rock – St. Barths
Spencer's family own this exclusive ultra luxe boutique hotel resort situated in the gorgeous bay of St Jean – you may even spot Spenny going for a paddle!
edenrockhotel.com

VERBIER

★

The winter haunt of the rich and famous.

When Andy organised a last-minute trip, it was no surprise that Jamie and co didn't have to think twice about slipping into their salopettes. Located in the Valais region of Switzerland, 'Verbs' (as it's known by Chelsea types) is a picturesque journey from Geneva airport. The lively nightlife is as legendary as the skiing, or you can just sample the buoyant aprés-ski bars in your ski boots and finish the evening feasting in your chalet. With 95 pistes for all abilities to choose from, the resort's more challenging runs gave adventurous Andy the chance to show off his epic ski technique.

★ ★ ★ ★ ★

PARTY
Pub Mont Fort
Check out the boisterous shots bar in the cellar of this legendary drinking hole – just make sure you've got a friend to carry you home!
pubmontfort.com

STAY
Chalet Maurine
You too can enjoy 'flirty fondue' and have a Jamie-style hot-tub experience by hiring the same chalet the gang stayed in – it sleeps 16 and is nestled in the heart of Verbier.
skiverbier.com

Here's

ROSIE FORTESCUE

'There was a language teacher
with self-confidence issues,
so we threw condoms at him.'

I was well-behaved at school... until sixth form when the misbehaving, drinking and smoking started. We were just so blasé about the rules by then because there was a big pack mentality (which included Louise from the show), so you could all get into trouble and there wasn't one person who could be blamed for it. We were so rude, no one wanted to teach us. There was a language teacher who had really bad self-confidence issues, so we threw condoms at him in the classroom.

I'm a twin... but my sister Lily is four inches taller with brown eyes and olive skin. She isn't pale like me and she's a lot louder. She's really lairy actually! There's no 'psychic thing' between us, but we do have each other's backs. Big time. If shit happens on the show, she gets really protective.

My guilty pleasure... is crunchy peanut butter, eaten with a spoon from the jar. I could easily eat half a jar in one sitting, and if it's in the flat, it's not going to be long for this world. Plus I have a Waitrose on my doorstep, so I am always popping out for more. It's unacceptable how much peanut butter I can eat.

We destroyed our au pairs... my sister and I caused a lot of trouble at home. We'd gang up on our au pairs and try to force them to quit with things like fake dog poo and fake dog sick. We had so many, my mum gets really embarrassed when I talk about it. We must've got through at least 10 or 15 of them.

Here's

FRANCIS BOULLE

'I like causing chaos and observing
the fallout. It keeps me amused anyway.'

I'm a notorious prankster... at The Oratory there's a thing called
Prank Week and everyone gets very creative, much to the annoyance
of the teachers. In advance the headmaster used to strategically
suspend the people they thought would do the worst pranks – but
I wasn't having any of it, so I snuck back in with seven thousand
crickets, beetles and locusts and let them loose in the atrium of one
of the boarding houses. It was like the whole floor was moving and
they actually went under the floorboards in the master's dining room
and started breeding. The school had to call in the exterminators
because you could still hear them in there three weeks later.

I hooked up with a girl dressed as a corn on the cob... I was
in Durham meeting up with friends who were at university there
and I met her in a club. I have no idea why she was dressed like that.
We went back to her hotel room and got walked in on by her friends
who were dressed as other vegetables.

On the show I am... a hybrid of being the voice of reason and
playful shit-stirring. I quite like causing chaos and observing the
fallout. It keeps me amused anyway.

I'm a massive Oasis fan... I once bumped into Liam when I was
coming out of the loo at a launch. I spotted him, so I said: 'I'm a
really big fan.' He replied: 'I'm a really big fan of your's, man. Where's
your wand?' I told him I wasn't a magician, then he asked if I was
going to go on a 'wander'. He may have thought I was Harry Potter.

CHRISTMAS

EAT, DRINK AND BE MERRY

Here's your guide to Christmas in the capital...

SHOP
Never mind what's inside, the dazzling window displays at Selfridges and Fortnum & Mason are worth a trip in themselves. When you have Christmas-shopped 'til you've dropped, treat yourself to afternoon tea at Fortnum's Diamond Jubilee Tea Salon or dinner at Selfridges' Corner Restaurant & Champagne Bar – run by Keri Moss, joint winner of *MasterChef* 2012.
fortnumandmason.com
selfridges.com

66 Christmas pud, mulled wine and chunky knitwear – it's so the best time of the year! 99 OLIVIA

SING
There's nothing like a spot of carolling to put yourself in the festive mood, and locations don't come much better than around the giant glittering Norwegian Christmas tree in the heart of Trafalgar Square. Join in with the sing-along each evening from mid-December in aid of various voluntary and charitable organisations.
london.gov.uk

DRINK
Who needs to go to Lapland when you can enjoy authentic Scandi cocktails and traditional *köttbullar* meatballs at Soho's cool and cosy Nordic Bar. Put yourself in a merry mood with their signature 'Snowflake' concoction – Tia Maria, schnapps and Baileys blended with fresh cream over ice.
nordicbar.com

RUN

Imagine an egg and spoon race with puds and you get Covent Garden's Great Christmas Pudding Race! It involves contestants in teams of six dashing around the piazza while trying to balance a Christmas pudding on a party plate. The fun event has been running since 1980 and is held for charity.
xmaspuddingrace.org.uk

EAT

The Southbank Centre's Christmas Chocolate Festival is the perfect place to indulge on the wares of the world's best chocolatiers and buy choc-tastic stocking fillers. Also check out the South Bank's German Christmas Market where you can take the edge off the winter chill with warming *glühwein* (mulled wine) and traditional bratwurst.
southbankcentre.co.uk

SWIM

The *Peter Pan* Cup Race, a Christmas-morning swim around Hyde Park's icy Serpentine Lake, has been an annual fixture since 1864. The race's name harks back to when *Peter Pan* author J.M. Barrie presented the very first trophy. The 9 a.m. start may be a tad early for some, but the event attracts an enthusiastic crowd and the park's wintry scenery is guaranteed to make you come over all Christmassy.
serpentineswimmingclub.com

WATCH

Every year hundreds of thousands of spectators gather on the banks of the Thames to enjoy London's spectacular New Year's Eve Fireworks. In 2012 rockets flared from the London Eye and a whopping 12,500 fireworks lit up the sky for miles around. The best views are from the South Bank, Victoria Embankment, Waterloo Bridge and Westminster Bridge.
london.gov.uk

"London at Christmas is like unwrapping the best present ever." JAMIE

189

MERRY KISS-MAS!

★

Smooching under the mistletoe: The Rules.

BE POLITE...
ask first. There's nothing worse than a total stranger suddenly lunging at you under the mistletoe.

KISS CORRECTLY...
peck the right cheek followed by the left. Then thank the other person and wish them a Merry Christmas.

BOYS, NEVER ATTACH MISTLETOE TO YOUR TROUSERS...
you may find it hilarious, but everyone else will think you're totes tradge.

REJECTING A MISTLETOE KISS IS FROWNED UPON...
it's all part of the festive fun and sometimes you just have to grin and bear it!

DON'T INVADE PERSONAL SPACE...
hands on shoulders and upper arms are fine, but anywhere else is just awkward.

Top Tip

Fran says:
'If you spot someone you're not interested in who's switching furtive glances between you and the mistletoe, politely excuse yourself and head for a glass of champagne. Similarly, if you find someone you do like, don't spend all night hanging about under the mistletoe – they'll sense your desperation. Be confident and flirty and that Christmas kiss will be yours!'

★ ★ ★

GIFT-GIVING
A FIVE-POINT PLAN

1 Always get a receipt... the other person will thank you for it and they can exchange it guilt-free.

2 Don't buy something just because *you* love it. You may want a Stella McCartney clutch, but your boyfriend probably doesn't.

3 Do your research... if you're stuck for ideas, ask what the recipient wants. It demonstrates you're a thoughtful person.

4 Size isn't important... it's not the hugeness of the box that defines the perfect gift, it's how much the person receiving it will love it.

5 Similarly, it's the thought that counts... not how much you've spent. The fact that you've bothered means more than any price tag.

GET YOUR SKATES ON

★

*Do your best Torvill and Dean twirl (or take a tumble)
at some of London's premier landmarks...*

NATURAL HISTORY MUSEUM
The towers of this iconic South Kensington building provide a magnificent backdrop. There's a café bar for 'aprés-skate' mulled wine too.
nhmskating.com

SOMERSET HOUSE
The 18th-century courtyard with its Tiffany-decorated tree makes this London's most glamorous ice rink. Book in for a late-night session of skating along to a soundtrack by top DJs.
somersethouse.org.uk

HAMPTON COURT PALACE
Skate into your very own fairy tale in this magical setting. Recommended at night when the royal palace is illuminated.
hamptoncourticerink.com

Here's

FRANCESCA NEWMAN-YOUNG

'I was one of those kids who would kick and scream on shop floors until I got what I wanted.'

I was a nightmare child... from the moment I could talk I was a massive attention-seeker and would be awful to my mother. I was one of those kids who would kick and scream on shop floors until I got what I wanted. I calmed down after I left school. I didn't like being told what to do, basically, so when I got my freedom I chilled out a bit.

I spent a lot of time sitting outside the classroom... I was the worst brat ever. I locked a teacher in a cupboard, I put a sweet-wrapper down a teacher's trousers (while he was still wearing them) and once I broke into a teacher's flat. He said if I didn't get my homework to him before he went to bed, then I'd be in serious trouble. So I put my homework in his bed. He didn't like that. I had to go to an educational psychologist to see if I had some kind of attention deficit disorder – but it turned out I was just bored.

I still have a massive temper... items fly, things get broken, doors slam. I like to kick things, but it's always me that ends up in pain rather than anyone else. It doesn't happen as often these days, but when it does, boyfriends usually get the brunt of it.

My claim to fame is... I was on the front page of the *Surrey Advertiser* when I was eight years old. My hamster, Coco, crawled inside one of our wooden beams – middle-class problem, I know – so being an *Animal Hospital* addict I immediately called the fire brigade and they coaxed him down with a peanut. It wasn't my best era when it came to style – it looks like I've got a monobrow in the photo.

Here's

JOSH COOMBS

'I loved Mr Blobby so much I convinced myself he recognised me.'

I was an adventurous child... I was never inside. Staying indoors would drive me insane, so I had to be out doing something, whether it was skateboarding, surfing or playing around on my BMX. I managed to sustain quite a few injuries along the way, including breaking my little finger, snapping my toe and cracking my collarbone while attempting a jump on my bike. The bone popped out so much my shoulder looked like a doorstep. My legs are still covered in scars even now.

I idolised Mr Blobby... I think it all started when my grandmother took me to his Blobbyland theme park for the first time. That kicked off my obsession. I had his record and all around the house there were pictures of me with him. I loved him so much that every time I went back to Blobbyland and had my photo taken with him I convinced myself he recognised me.

Music is my passion... I'm a DJ as well as being a freelance designer. I like to play music that makes people happy. Sometimes it has gone so well that I've had propositions from girls who want to come into the DJ booth and get to know me better, which is just a bit awkward and wrong.

My guilty pleasure is... the spa. I love a full-on girlie day at somewhere like Babington House where I can be pampered and indulged. Massages, facials, mud-packs, I do them all. I just wish I could be carried from one treatment to the next because I get so relaxed that even going for a massage feels a bit of a strain.

CHELSEA
HANGOUTS

GOING OUT

Want to dine like Spencer, drink like Francis and pardy like Jamie and Binky? Here the *Made in Chelsea* gang reveal their secret hangouts for the very first time. Ssshhh, don't tell anyone...

★ BEST FOR ROMANCE ★

DAPHNE'S

112 Draycott Ave, SW3 3AE
Chelsea chap Mark Francis has been coming here all his life. Chic, discreet and relaxed, Daphne's is romance and Italian food personified.
daphnes-restaurant.co.uk

EIGHT OVER EIGHT

392 King's Road, SW3 5UZ
Inventive Pan-Asian cuisine in an elegant environment. Cheska reckons it's the perfect place to fall in love.
rickerrestaurants.com

THE WOLSELEY

160 Piccadilly, W1J 9EB
With its sparkling chandeliers and attentive service, this bustling grand café couldn't be more romantic for breakfast, lunch or dinner. Rosie loves it.
thewolseley.com

★ BEST FOR BRUNCH ★

BLUEBIRD CHELSEA

350 King's Road, SW3 5UU
Stylish neighbourhood bar-restaurant that has been the scene of many an awkward *Made in Chelsea* catch-up. Millie's a sucker for the Eggs Benedict and Bucks Fizz. *bluebird-restaurant.co.uk*

JOE'S BRASSERIE

130 Wandsworth Bridge Road, SW6 2UL
Perfect for a weekend full English breakfast or their signature smoked chicken hash – you might even spot regular customer Andy in there! *brinkleys.com*

MEGAN'S RESTAURANT & DELI

571 King's Road, SW6 2EB
Hearty home-style cooking. Binky swears by the spinach, Parma ham, poached egg and Hollandaise sauce and toast. *megansrestaurant.com*

PJ'S BAR & GRILL

52 Fulham Road, SW3 6HH
Polo-themed Chelsea institution. Jamie loves their extensive brunch menu and recommends the delish chicken club sandwich with fries. *pjsbarandgrill.co.uk*

THE TROUBADOUR

263–267 Old Brompton Road, SW5 9JA
A Cheska hangout and the location of Caggie's very first gig. Tuck into the sizeable 'Reviver' fry-up for all your hangover needs. *troubadour.co.uk*

VINGT-QUATRE

325 Fulham Road, SW10 9QL
Buzzing 24-hour café and diner that, according to Spencer, serves the best Eggs Benedict in London. *vq24hours.com*

★ BEST FOR A FOODIE FIRST DATE ★

BIG EASY

332–334 King's Road, SW3 5UR Enjoy a stress-free date at this fun barbecue and crab-shack. Keep an eye out for Ollie and Cheska tucking into the signature USA-style ribs and lobster.
bigeasy.co.uk

COYA

118 Piccadilly, W1J 7NW Stylish Peruvian cooking. Try smoked dishes from the traditional 'Josper' oven, washed down with a watermelon martini. Victoria is Coya's No 1 fan.
coyarestaurant.com

YAUATCHA

15–17 Broadwick Street, W1F 0DL This sleekly designed, Soho dim-sum hangout is Proudlock's favourite eatery. The Shanghai dumplings and sticky vegetable puffs are perfect for sharing!
yauatcha.com

ZUMA

5 Raphael St, SW7 1DL Jamie's favourite Japanese joint. Famed for its Green tea and banana cake with coconut ice cream and peanut toffee sauce. Two spoons, please!
zumarestaurant.com

★ BEST BARS ★

AMUSE BOUCHE

51 Parsons Green Lane, SW6 4JA Champagne served by the glass in unpretentious modern surroundings. Stevie is a fan, and it was also the scene of a random Andy and Binky catch-up. *amusebouchelondon.com*

BARTS

87 Sloane Ave, SW3 3DW This quirky but cool speakeasy-styled bar is hidden behind a discreet black door. Ideal for late-night drinking – try the 'Pickled Ploughman' made with gin and ... Stilton! *barts-london.com*

JUJU

316–318 King's Road, SW3 5UH Stylish regular haunt of the *Made in Chelsea* posse (Gabriella had her birthday party there) and winner of a Best Late Night Bar Award for 2013. *jujulondon.com*

MEURSAULT

36 Gloucester Road, SW7 4QT The scene of Lucy and Andy's first date and a *Made in Chelsea* drinkies favourite – the shared sashimi nibbles (try saying that after a few cocktails) are delish. *meursaultlondon.co.uk*

TONTERIA

7 12 Sloane Square, SW1W 8EG Princes Harry and Wills love it and you might even spot Olivia necking the tequila (and the yummy nibbles) at this kitsch yet classy Mexican-themed joint. *tonteria.co.uk*

★ BEST BOOZERS ★

THE ANGLESEA ARMS

15 Selwood Terrace, SW7 3QG
Traditional pub with a laidback vibe – watch out for Francis supping a pint as he puts the finishing touches to his latest bestseller.
capitalpubcompany.com

THE THOMAS CUBITT

44 Elizabeth St, SW1W 9PA
A Spencer haunt, this classic country-house-style pub has a buzzy atmosphere and a much-heralded restaurant.
thethomascubitt.co.uk

THE JAM TREE

541 King's Road, London, SW6 2EB
This gastro pub is a *Made in Chelsea* favourite – if it's sunny you might spot Millie and Rosie sitting outside enjoying a bottle of rosé.
thejamtree.com

THE WHITE HORSE

1–3 Parsons Green, SW6 4UL
Cosy, traditional-style gastro pub that is popular with Stevie and Andy. There's a huge selection of ales and the venue hosts regular beer festivals.
whitehorsesw6.com

THE PHENE

9 Phene St, SW3 5NY
Owned by Lucy's dad and the scene of the cringe confrontation between Lucy and Phoebe over Alex. The best spots are in the stunning heated beer garden.
thephene.com

★ BEST FOR COFFEE ★

GAIL'S

341 Fulham Road, SW10 9TW
A morning cup of smooth Gail's coffee is a Fulham must-do – Andy likes his with a little biccie on the side.
gailsbread.co.uk

JOE & THE JUICE

65 King's Road, SW3 4NT
The King's Road branch of this Danish chain is a cast favourite – their lattes may even be the best in south west London.
joejuice.com

LADURÉE AT HARRODS

87/135 Brompton Road, Harrod's entrance on Hans Road, SW1X 7XL
The Parisian chain's flagship store is a coffee and cake-lover's dream. The tables outside are where Victoria positions herself for the best people-watching.
laduree.com

★ BEST FOR A ROAST ★

BUMPKIN

102 Old Brompton Road, SW7 3RD Spencer and Cheska swear by Bumpkin's UK-sourced Sunday roasts – served with all the trimmings and lashings of gravy. *bumpkinuk.com*

THE BROWN COW

676 Fulham Road, SW6 5SA A light and airy dog-friendly pub, popular with Binky, Andy and Stevie (who loves their Yorkshire puddings). *thebrowncowpub.co.uk*

THE PANTECHNICON

10 Motcomb Street, SW1X 8LA Francis's No 1 Sunday dining destination offers organic roasts and hearty puds, such as a fig tart with gingerbread ice cream. *thepantechnicon.com*

THE PIG'S EAR

35 Old Church Street, SW3 5BS This award-winning gastro-pub is Millie's favoured Sunday lunch venue – you can even munch on a crispy pig's ear as your starter. *thepigsear.info*

★ BEST FOR COCKTAILS ★

ECLIPSE

111–113 Walton Street, SW3 2HP
The vibrant bar scene on Walton Street is ideal for a cocktail-fuelled stagger. Eclipse is a *Made in Chelsea* gang favourite. Try The Eclipse, the bar's signature watermelon martini.
eclipsebars.com

EIGHTY-SIX

86 Fulham Road, SW3 6HR
Binky recommends the restaurant's glamorous gallery bar. Check out the triple-rum-based Zombie or the Classic Champagne Cocktail.
86restaurant.co.uk

THE BLUE BAR

The Berkeley, Wilton Place,
SW1X 7RL
Romantic and (surprise, surprise) blue-themed hotel bar the decor, the service and the cocktails are pure sophistication. Nominated by Victoria.
the-berkeley.co.uk

THE EXPERIMENTAL COCKTAIL CLUB

13a Gerrard Street, W1D 5PS
It's no surprise that Proudlock is a regular mojito drinker at this cool and arty Chinatown joint. Book a table in advance.
chinatownecc.com

THE RUM KITCHEN

6–8 All Saints Road, W11 1HH
Caribbean-inspired cocktail bar and restaurant in the heart of Notting Hill – see if you can spot Olivia slurping on a Pina Colada.
therumkitchen.com

★ BEST FOR LUNCH WITH MUM ★

BEACH BLANKET BABYLON
45 Ledbury Road, W11 2AA
Quirkily designed restaurant
favoured by Cheska and her mum.
Puds such as vanilla pod cheesecake
and a warm chocolate brownie
are heard to beat.
beachblanket.co.uk

BISTRO ONE NINETY

*190 Queen's Gate,
SW7 5EX*
Lively all-day
eatery in South
Kensington's The Gore hotel –
where Spencer and Jamie
enjoyed a carving lesson.
gorehotel.com

CECCONI'S
5A Burlington Gardens, W1S 3EP
Venetian-inspired food in elegant
surroundings right in the heart of
Mayfair. According to Jamie, their
chicken salad is the best in London!
cecconis.co.uk

LA BRASSERIE
272 Brompton Road, SW3 2AW
This bustling informal bistro is
Proudlock's choice for lunch with
mum Lena. Founded over 40
years ago, it's the perfect place
to people-watch.
labrasserielondon.com

★ BEST FOR NIGHTLIFE ★

BOUJIS

*43 Thurloe Street,
SW7 2LQ*
Kate and Wills
have been papped
leaving this hallowed Chelsea
members' club, but these days
you'll have to make do with Spencer
throwing some moves instead!
boujis.com

MAGGIE'S

*329 Fulham Road,
SW10 9QL*
Fun 80s-themed
nightclub inspired
by Mrs Thatcher (yes, really). Her
speeches are played on repeat in
the loo. Binky's choice for a girls'
night out.
maggies-club.com

★ THE BEST OF THE REST ★

ARCHER STREET
Cool and comfy Soho bar.
archerstreet.co.uk

CADOGAN ARMS
Likeable King's Road gastro pub.
thecadoganarmschelsea.com

BABBLE
Mayfair cocktail bar and club.
babble-bar.co.uk

CIRCUS
Pan-Asian restaurant and cabaret.
circus-london.co.uk

BEAUFORT HOUSE
Brasserie and members' club.
beauforthousechelsea.co.uk

DIRTY MARTINI
Mayfair cocktail bar.
dirtymartini.uk.com

BROADWAY HOUSE
Fulham-based members' club.
broadway-house.com

DOODLE BAR
Chill-out doodling venue.
thedoodlebar.com

★ **DOODLE BAR** ★

EMBARGO 59
Opulent bar and nightclub.
embargo59.com

HENRY ROOT
Friendly neighbourhood bistro
and bar.
thehenryroot.com

HUSH
Chic informal dining.
hush.co.uk

IBÉRICA MARYLEBONE
Contemporary tapas restaurant.
ibericalondon.co.uk

JALOUSE
Hanover Square members' club.
jalouse.co.uk

KENSINGTON ROOF GARDENS
Unique restaurant and club.
roofgardens.virgin.com

LE CAFÉ ANGLAIS
Award-winning French bistro.
lecafeanglais.co.uk

LE CERCLE
Modern French restaurant.
lecercle.co.uk

★ **IBÉRICA MARYLEBONE** ★

MADISON BAR
Rooftop tapas and cocktails.
madisonlondon.net

MAZE
French/Asian fusion restaurant.
gordonramsay.com/maze

NIKITA'S
Stylish Russian cuisine.
nikitasrestaurant.co.uk

NOIR BAR
Cosy Fitzrovia cocktail bar.
noirbar.com

NO 11 CADOGAN GARDENS
Smart hotel restaurant-bar.
no11cadogangardens.com

NO 11 PIMLICO ROAD
Relaxed all-day eatery.
no11pimlicoroad.co.uk

SMITH'S BAR & GRILL
Informal Paddington restaurant.
smithsbarandgrill.co.uk

SUSHI DES ARTISTES
Upmarket Japanese restaurant.
sushidesartistes.com

★ **NO 11 CADOGAN GARDENS** ★

THE CHELSEA RAM
Classy gastro-pub grub.
geronimo-inns.co.uk

THE GRAZING GOAT
Elegant pub and hotel.
thegrazinggoat.co.uk

THE HOLLYWOOD ARMS
Luxurious British-style eatery.
hollywoodarmschelsea.com

THE STAR TAVERN
Award-winning Belgravia pub.
star-tavern-belgravia.co.uk

THIRTY SIX
Refined British cuisine.
dukeshotel.com

TOM'S KITCHEN
Modern British brasserie.
tomskitchen.co.uk

UPPER WEST
NYC-inspired bar and roof garden.
upperwestlondon.com

VISTA BAR
Bar overlooking Trafalgar Square.
thetrafalgar.com

★ **TOM'S KITCHEN** ★

213

Here's

OLIVIA NEWMAN-YOUNG

'I got into clubs in Ibiza for free because they thought I was Paris Hilton.'

I had a crush on Steven Tyler... when I was younger I would lie in bed with my eyes closed listening to Aerosmith on my Discman, pretending I was his girlfriend going to a gig. God only knows what I was thinking. I'm not quite so into him now – the blow-dried old-lady hair has put me off a bit.

My claim to fame is... I used to get into clubs in Ibiza for free because they thought I was Paris Hilton. They also thought my friend was Usher. Obviously a lot of the people there were likely to be off their tits, but they'd come up to me taking photos on their phones going, 'Paris, I love you!'. So I just went along with it. I'd pose for pictures but at the same time I'd be laughing to myself, thinking: 'Just wait until you look at these photos properly tomorrow!'

I've smeared make-up onto horses... I worked as a make-up artist on the film *War Horse* and met Steven Spielberg. As well as seeing to about 200 extras we had to apply make-up to the horses, which involved getting up at four in the morning in the middle of winter, wearing ski gear in an attempt to keep warm and rubbing fake mud onto each horse, because for health and safety reasons we couldn't use the real stuff. It was horrific – and people think the film industry is glamorous.

My passion is cooking... I left school after my AS-levels and trained to be a Cordon Bleu chef. We'd make pastries, fish dishes, debone chickens and cook a three-course meal every day – I got very fat, obviously!

CHELSEA
SLANG

CHELSEA SLANG

Master these key words and phrases
and you'll be chatting like a true
Chelsea-ite in no time...

Amazeballs *adj*
Popularised via Twitter
(#amazeballs), used to confirm
both surprise and delight at
the same time. 'Binky's hair
is amazeballs.'

Awesome *adj*
A thing that inspires awe and
wonder. For true Chelsea usage,
apply to an item that would
normally be considered mundane.
'Dude, this frothy latte is *awesome*.'

Awkward! *Adj*
A moment of discomfort at
one's surroundings. For example,
Spencer inviting ex-girlfriend
Lucy Watson and her new beau
Alex to his villa in Barcelona.
'Awkward!'

Bois *n*
A close male friend, said with
emphasis on the 'oi' sound.
Also used as a greeting,
usually repeated endlessly
and inexplicably. 'I know
Spencer and I have our tiffs,
but he's still my boi.'

Dorbs *adj*
From 'adorable'. Used to describe
something or someone of cute
status. 'Have you seen Cheska's
doggie? She's totes dorbs!'

Epic *adj*
Great. Off the scale brilliance.
Often used to describe an event
or occurrence of jaw-dropping
standards. 'Dude, you should've
been at Stevie's house-party last
night – it was epic!'

'Getting up in my grill' *phrase*
When somebody is annoying you, pestering you, or just generally getting your goat. Favoured by Lucy when questioned about her behaviour at Rosie's dinner party.

'It's not a look!' *phrase*
Judgement on another's personal appearance. Used regularly by Chelsea critic Mark Francis. 'Victoria, have you seen Jamie's leopard-print t-shirt? It's not a look!'

Jokes *adj*
Cool. Again favoured by imaginative linguist Proudlock.

Little one *n*
Alternative name for Louise, preferred by Chelsea Head Girl Rosie. Derives from Louise's diminutive state.

Pardy *n; v*
A gathering of people, normally involving music, drink and overwhelming amounts of awkward encounters. Pronounced with a 'd' for correct use. Also used as a verb to describe one's plans to enjoy oneself. 'Tonight we are going to pardy haaaaard!'

Rank *adj*
How one describes something of an unpleasant and vulgar nature. 'Have you seen her faux Louis Vuitton clutch? It's fifty shades of rank.'

'Sacked me off' *phrase*
To reject someone. 'Lucy sacked me off when she dumped me during dinner.'

Savage *adj*
Ruthless and heartless behaviour. Use to describe a particularly brutal relationship rejection. To 'Lucy dumped me before I'd even ordered my starter' the reply would be 'Savage!'.

Schoolboy *n; adj*
Abbreviation of the phrase
'schoolboy error'. Used to
describe a move of fundamental
foolishness. 'You left your phone
in a room with your girlfriend,
unlocked? Schoolboy!'

Shweffing *v*
Trying to get with girls at the
expense of boi time. 'Andy's
such a shweff – his poor
chum Stevie barely sees him.'

Sick *adj*
Cool, fashionable, enjoyable.
Mostly popularised by resident
fop Proudlock to describe his
latest venture. 'My fashion
designs are sick.'

Totes *adj*
From the word 'totally'. A term
of agreement or emphasis without
the tiresome and unnecessary
second and third syllables. 'Jamie
getting into a hot tub is a totes
bad idea.'

Yaaa *n*
Derives from the popular word
'yes'. Can be used at the end of
practically every sentence, yaaa?
Normally with upwards intonation
to suggest a question that demands
no answer…yaaa?

ELOCUTION LESSONS

★

Here's how to achieve that perfect Chelsea twang...

DON'T VOWEL IT UP

Absolutely no flat vowels will do. If you're
laffing and not larrrfing, you've blown your
non-Chelsea cover.

MAKE IT QUIZZICAL?

A sentence should never end with an absolute
full stop. Remember to send your final syllable
sky high with a tone that sounds like a...
question? Even when it's... not?

PRONUNCIATION

Some phonetic examples to help you master that accent:

'Spuncuh und Undah wunt for a wark on the Kung's Rurd.'
'Spencer and Andy went for a walk on the King's Road.'

★

'Us it jarst me or was Luhweeze rally butchy to me jarst now?'
'Is it just me or was Louise really bitchy to me just now?'

★

The author would like to thank
Heidi Birkett and Poppy
Almond at Monkey Kingdom.

The publishers would like
to thank Nick Young at NBC
Universal and Rebecca Turner
at Channel 4 for all their help
in putting this book together.

★

2 4 6 8 10 9 7 5 3 1

First published in 2013 by Virgin Books, an imprint of Ebury Publishing

A Random House Group Company

Addresses for companies within The Random House Group Limited can be found
at www.randomhouse.co.uk/offices.htm

The Random House Group Limited Reg. No. 954009

A CIP catalogue record for this book is available from the British Library

The Random House Group Limited supports the Forest Stewardship Council® (FSC®), the leading
international forest-certification organisation. Our books carrying the FSC label are printed on FSC®-
certified paper. FSC is the only forest-certification scheme supported by the leading environmental
organisations, including Greenpeace. Our paper procurement policy can be found at
www.randomhouse.co.uk/environment

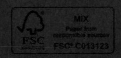

Design by Smith & Gilmour
Illustrations by Sarah Hankinson

Photography on pages 2, 21, 23, 39, 41, 42, 43, 45, 46, 58, 97, 103, 104, 105, 107, 111, 114, 119, 139, 171,
185, 195, 209, 215, 222 by Sam Spurgeon

Photography on pages 32, 65, 66, 69, 70, 74, 77, 78, 109, 173 by Pete Dadds

Photography on pages 10, 11, 59, 61, 99, 121, 141, 157, 159, 183, 197 © Monkey Kingdom Ltd

Images on pages 5, 8, 24, 35, 37, 62, 86, 88, 100, 117, 126, 142, 160, 167, 168, 174, 186, 198 © Shutterstock

51 Piers Allardyce/Rex, 73 Dave M. Benett/Getty Images, 87 Rex, 131 Valery Hache/AFP/Getty Images,
132 Rainer W. Schlegelmilch/Getty Images, 145 Chris Jackson/Getty Images, 146 Ian Walton/Getty Images,
149 Andreas Rentz/Getty Images, 151 Getty Images for Aberdeen Asset Management, 153 by Gareth Howell,
165 Dan Kitwood/Getty Images, 169 Aime Reina/AFP/Getty Images, 193 George Rose/Getty Images

Printed and bound in Italy by Graphicom SRL

ISBN: 9780753541920

To buy books by your favourite authors and register for offers, visit www.randomhouse.co.uk